Reginald Shepherd

A Martian Muse

FURTHER ESSAYS ON IDENTITY, POLITICS, AND THE FREEDOM OF POETRY

Edited and with an Introduction by
Robert Philen

THE UNIVERSITY OF MICHIGAN PRESS
Ann Arbor

Published in the United States of America by
The University of Michigan Press
Manufactured in the United States of America
∞ Printed on acid-free paper

2013 2012 2011 2010 4 3 2 1

A CIP catalog record for this book is available from the British Library.

Library of Congress Cataloging-in-Publication Data

Shepherd, Reginald, 1963–2008
A Martian muse : further essays on identity, politics, and the freedom of poetry / Reginald Shepherd ; edited and with an introduction by Robert Philen.
p. cm. — (Poets on poetry)
ISBN 978-0-472-07097-8 (cloth : alk. paper) —
ISBN 978-0-472-05097-0 (pbk. : alk. paper)
1. Shepherd, Reginald, 1963–2008 2. Poetry—Authorship.
3. Poetics. 4. Politics and literature. I. Philen, Robert.
II. Title. III. Series.

PS3569.H3967Z46 2010
811'.54—dc22 2009047785

A Martian Muse

POETS ON POETRY

Annie Finch and Marilyn Hacker, General Editors
Donald Hall, Founding Editor

New titles

Meena Alexander, *Poetics of Dislocation*
Sandra M. Gilbert, *On Burning Ground: Thirty Years of Thinking About Poetry*
Grace Schulman, *First Loves and Other Adventures*
Reginald Shepherd, *Orpheus in the Bronx*
Reginald Shepherd, *A Martian Muse: Further Essays on Identity, Politics, and the Freedom of Poetry*

Recently published

Elizabeth Alexander, *Power and Possibility*
Alfred Corn, *Atlas*
Ed Dorn, *Ed Dorn Live*
Annie Finch, *The Body of Poetry*

Also available, collections by

A. R. Ammons, John Ashbery, Robert Bly, Philip Booth, Marianne Boruch, Hayden Carruth, Amy Clampitt, Douglas Crase, Robert Creeley, Donald Davie, Thomas M. Disch, Tess Gallagher, Dana Gioia, Linda Gregerson, Allen Grossman, Thom Gunn, Rachel Hadas, John Haines, Donald Hall, Joy Harjo, Robert Hayden, Edward Hirsch, Daniel Hoffman, Jonathan Holden, John Hollander, Paul Hoover, Andrew Hudgins, Laura (Riding) Jackson, Josephine Jacobsen, Mark Jarman, Galway Kinnell, Kenneth Koch, John Koethe, Yusef Komunyakaa, Maxine Kumin, Martin Lammon (editor), Philip Larkin, David Lehman, Philip Levine, Larry Levis, John Logan, William Logan, William Matthews, William Meredith, Jane Miller, David Mura, Carol Muske, Alice Notley, Geoffrey O'Brien, Gregory Orr, Alicia Suskin Ostriker, Ron Padgett, Marge Piercy, Anne Sexton, Karl Shapiro, Charles Simic, William Stafford, Anne Stevenson, May Swenson, James Tate, Richard Tillinghast, C. K. Williams, Alan Williamson, Charles Wright, James Wright, John Yau, and Stephen Yenser

Contents

Artistic Production

Intention, Aspiration, Inspiration

Illness, Identity, and Poetry

Introduction

Robert Philen

Reginald Shepherd died September 10, 2008, after a hard struggle with cancer. While he had completed the essays presented here and had selected them from his available essays to form a collection, he didn't have time to organize the presentation of the essays within the collection.

The task of editing this collection has been a daunting challenge as I struggle to live up to the level of intellectual engagement, clarity, and coherence that Reginald always expected. While daunting, it has also been a labor of love and a compulsion for me, based on the many years I spent with him as partner, friend, lover, intellectual companion, and sharer of common passions.

All of the essays are Reginald's finished products. Even while the editing of the collection as a whole has been difficult (not because the essays are lacking in clarity, coherency, or connections, but because the pressure I feel to get things right is so high), at the level of the individual essay, at least, Reginald made things easy for me. I've made, and needed to make, only minor alterations to his texts, none of which affect the sense of his arguments.

I've added a few essays to Reginald's original collection. These are the series of short pieces addressing illness, identity, and poetry in the final section of the book. They were written over his last few months, when he was seriously ill. In his final weeks, we discussed making this addition, and it is a change he intended to make to the collection if he had had the opportunity.

My main editing intervention has been in the discernment and imposition of order upon the collection of essays. I can't say with certainty that this is exactly how he would have organized the book, but I know him well enough to be confident he'd be happy with it.

In the months since Reginald's death, I've revisited and reread most all of his writing, poetry, and prose, at least a time or two. One piece I've returned to repeatedly is the short essay, included in this collection, "Taking Dictation from a Martian Muse," in which he treats the notion of poetry as derived from the muses in a variety of guises, though focusing especially on Jack Spicer's notion of poetry as dictation.

Reginald was largely skeptical of the idea of poetry as dictation, derived from Muses, or transmissions from Cocteau's Orphée's ghost radio:

> Interesting and even inspiring though Spicer's notion of dictation is, with its promise of escaping what he calls "the big lie of the personal," I wonder if it's not simply the mirror image of romantic inspiration. Instead of coming from deep within one, from one's soul or innermost self, the poem comes from outside one, from the Martians or the spooks. In either case, the poet is passive, and abdicates thought and responsibility. . . . Spicer's Martians seem to be the Muses dressed up in space suits, another way to preserve the romantic (small "r") notion of the poet as a specially inspired individual with access to the transcendent.

This is not at all to say that Reginald rejected the notion of poetry as inspired through something like a muse (whether one thinks of that in terms of Martians dictating, ghost radios, the workings of the subconscious mind, or musical possession):

> I like the idea of poetry as dictation, because writing does feel like that sometimes. I've had at least one poem that was literally dictated to me—I woke up and the poem was reciting itself in my head, though I had to come up with my own ending. Don't we all? In that sense Spicer conveys what it often feels like to do poetry.

I'd say it's more that Reginald felt that while muses may be involved in the process of writing poetry, they are not sufficient, for the poem requires the active working by the poet upon potentially poetic material, wherever that may have come from:

> The poem, when it is at its best, when we are at our best, is a kind of agon between the poet and the language, and the poet has to bring all his or her resources to bear, or it's not a real struggle at all, just a performance.

Reginald's penultimate* poem (if it may be called that) is a good example of the relation between muses and poetry, both in the sense of its writing being clearly *of* something other than his fully conscious, cogent mind, and in the sense that it's obviously not fully formed poetry.

In mid-April 2008, several months before he did die in September, Reginald almost died as a result of a perforated intestine, followed by massive abdominal infection and blood poisoning. He was unconscious for ten days in the Intensive Care Unit, with a ventilator down his throat, alongside many other tubes, lines, and pieces of equipment attached here and there to other parts of his body. Even when he regained consciousness, he was completely unable to talk until the ventilator tube was removed, and barely able to talk after that because of lack of strength. For a few days after regaining consciousness and having the ventilator tube removed, he had frequent hallucinations (the result of both the sedatives he had been on and his sickness) and slipped easily in and out of fully cogent consciousness even in moments when I don't think he was hallucinating.

Over the period of a few days during which he was in and out of consciousness but was largely unable to talk, Reginald communicated to me or to his ICU nurses by writing on a clipboard. Much of this writing is completely illegible, as he didn't have good motor control in his arms at that point. Much of what is legible is lacking in cogency (he was frequently hallucinating at the time, after all). Most of what is legible and cogent

---

**Editor's Note:* He wrote his final poem, "God-With-Us," in late August 2008, around the same time as he wrote the essay "Heaven Is a Place Where Nothing Ever Happens," both written from his hospital bed about two weeks before his death.

is fairly prosaic—parts of simple conversations I remember having with him (or that he had with one of the nurses), such as a short grocery list (grapes, juice, peeled apples, plums, jello) he wrote after I asked him if there was anything he wanted me to bring him.

But a few weeks ago, while looking through those papers (I hadn't looked through them much before, because they were too painful), I encountered this, written sometime the day after he regained consciousness, but when he was still frequently suffering powerful hallucinations and was only fully cogent for short moments:

for month and years [*,the?*] [*. . . etary?*] [*fruits?*]
[*frails?*]
and [*to end?*] her [*battle?*] many of other
[*toward?*] [*b. the?*] [*history?*]
[*into . . . ?*]
the single step and [*lags?*] distance
every [*curve follows, linking to above word*]
between [*L. mbe. g?*] and [ ]

a palmful of Persian peaches

~~No~~ the world is[s] a work of wish and

~~no~~ human ~~eire~~ circumstance

this history of being rusted, being burned
~~ben~~ rusting, being burned

the [*alval?*] [*bag?*] of of years burned up, not down

burned off [*to?*] the for night

The first part in particular is virtually impossible to decipher as a result of the quality of the handwriting, which improves over the course of the page—as if gaining strength and confidence as he wrote. (I would like to acknowledge the help of Brad Richard in attempts to fully decipher the text, to the extent that Reginald's handwritten page can be deciphered.) Nonetheless, as fragmentary as the text is, as indecipherable as parts of it unfortunately are, the form and elements of a poem are there on the page, and if this isn't dictation from a muse, I'm not sure what would be.

Overall, it's clear from his body of work that Reginald was extraordinarily sensitive to potential poetic material. Some of the material of his poetry consisted of linguistic "found objects," his noticing poetic uses of language whether they occurred in casual conversations or on roadside signs, but most of his material came to him as though from the muses, with Reginald always careful to note poetic material that occurred to him, such that he was constantly jotting things down in one little notebook or another. Maybe that's all that having a muse is—being attentive to powerful language as it occurs, or maybe Reginald was taking dictation from Martians, channeling transmissions from the ghost radio, or being periodically possessed by Muses. In any case, that was only the start. Regardless of the source of poetic material, he still had to pay attention and then engage in attentive work to create poems. In the process of creating his art, there really were multiple and largely distinct facets to Reginald Shepherd as poet—on the one hand the medium channeling inspiration and/or careful observer of language (in some cases he had whole lines and more "dictated" from somewhere that he had to write down quickly or lose them forever; in other cases [and more with those linguistic "found objects"] he was more like a particularly astute detective of language); on the other hand the artisan or craftsman who skillfully transformed raw poetic material into finished poetry.

In any case, it's difficult to figure out what to do with this penultimate poem of his. It's tempting to call it a poetic fragment and leave it as is, though with the caveat that this is a fragment in a different sense from textual fragments like Petronius's *Satyricon,* a completed text of which only fragments remain, whereas these are fragments of potentiality, artifacts of a poem never made, and it's precisely for that reason that I don't think Reginald would ultimately want the fragment left as is. It's also tempting to me to suppress it as an unfinished work (too late for that now, I suppose), but I don't think Reginald would want that either. There were works of his that he had chosen not to publish. He had a file titled "Poems not suitable for publication." Most of the poems in this file are quite good, just poems he didn't consider his best and/or poems he intended to go back to and work more with if he had time, such that it was really the case that he considered them poems not suitable for publication *yet.* Still, he didn't want those poems suppressed (something I know because I asked him about it specifically and explicitly on several occasions)—only not published until such point as there was no possibility of his working on them more. This "poem," written under such extraordinary circumstances, is more fragmentary than those other poems (which actually aren't fragmentary at all), but I don't think he'd want it suppressed, and in any case, I find it impossible to suppress lines like "a palmful of Persian peaches." Finally, it's tempting to work these fragments, engage in the agon between poet and language—a prospect I find frightening to say the least, though at least in this case, there is a legible and coherent core to the fragmentary text that with only minor editing and excision (rather than addition coming from me rather than Reginald) functions as a poem in its own right. Something like:

> A palmful of Persian peaches,
> the world is a work of wish and
> human circumstance,
> this history of being rusted, being burned
> rusting, being burned
> years burned up, not down
> burned off to the night

I'm not sure what Reginald would have ultimately done with his fragmentary text, given the chance, but I am confident of what his approach would have been—to have recognized it as material from the Muses that he would have further agonized with to create poetry.

The essays in *A Martian Muse,* reflecting the broad-ranging nature of Shepherd's mind, explore the big issues of any consideration of poetry, How poetry works, and How poetry is written or comes to be, though with each essay characterized by the precision and specificity that are a hallmark of his poetry and prose.

Shepherd was also interested in the relationship among poetry, the author, and society. As he made quite clear in his essays in *Orpheus in the Bronx,* Shepherd saw literature and art generally as autonomous practices not determined by the artist's biography or social circumstance. This did not mean that he thought art had no relationship to the artist's identity or society, as his explorations in this collection of the relation between art and society in the works of Paul Celan, Wilfred Owen, or Shakespeare should make clear. Instead, as can be seen in "Illness and Poetry," he insisted on recognizing the ways in which the individual's identity and art are not determined by biography or social circumstance, and that in any case such biographical facts are usually more multitudinous than often recognized. The fact that he lived with HIV for years certainly influenced him, and occasionally inspired brilliant poetry (see "Antibody" from his third poetry collection, *Wrong*). The facts of being HIV+, black, gay, raised in poverty in the Bronx, earning MFA degrees from Brown and Iowa, loving *Tristan und Isolde* (and many other operas), being continuously fascinated by figures from Greek mythology (Orpheus and Achilles in particular), spending eight and a half years with me—each of these strongly shaped him and his identity. As a result of a particular concatenation of such biographic facts that made him quite different from the average denizen of either the literary or the academic scene (most especially in terms of his class background), he often felt a profound sense of otherness in his identity and in his inspirations to write. To the extent he had a muse it often was as if a "Martian" muse.

But none of these things determined him or his poetry. Even among his most clearly "HIV poems," such as "Antibody," there are passages like these that have little clearly to do with HIV: "What's left of burning / burns as well: me down to blackened / glass, an offering in anthracite, / the darkest glitter smoldering underground / until it consumes the earth / which loves me anyway, I'm sure."

He also strongly rejected common notions of art as "elitist," or "oppressive," or straightforward reflection or instrument of capitalist imperialism. He noted elsewhere and in essays in this collection that for him growing up in poverty in the Bronx, art offered freedom from everyday oppression. As he put it himself in his introduction to *Orpheus in the Bronx,* "I have been oppressed by many things in my life, but not by literature, which enacts possibility rather than closure."

Robert Philen
February 2009

Poetics and Poetry

What We Talk About When We Talk About Poetry

1

When seen from a distance or just casually glanced at, poetry appears to be a substantive and singular thing. But when looked at more closely and attentively, this apparent unity dissolves: all that seemed solid melts into the air. As evidenced by the failure of all attempts at a comprehensive definition, we use the word "poetry" to refer to many different things. There is a nebulous family resemblance among these different things. But their attributes and aims are so distinct that it's hard to believe they are all "poetry" in the same sense.

Former British prime minister Margaret Thatcher once famously declared that there is no such thing as society; she was wrong. But there is no such single thing as poetry that does or should do a single thing or set of things. When we say, "This is what poetry is" or "This is what poetry does," we almost always mean, "This is what the kind of poetry that interests me is" or "This is what the kind of poetry that I like does." I know what I value in poems, what I want poems to do. But I also know that what I value isn't the definition of poetry, if only because there are so many poems that do other things, that aim at other goals. They can't all be dismissed as bad poems. Some of them certainly are; perhaps most are. But that's because they're badly done in their own terms, not because they don't match my definitions. They represent competing ideas of what poems are, of what poetry is. Ted Kooser, Barrett Watten, and, to take a poet from the tradition, Milton hardly seem to inhabit the same poetic universe at all. And yet all three are "poets," whatever adjectives one attaches to that noun.

In his piece "The End of History," which appeared as a post on the Poetry Foundation's "Harriet Blog" and was thus, perhaps, intended to be ephemeral, visual artist turned poet Kenny Goldsmith observes that "surveying the field, it appears to me to be wide open. Compared to the art world where, after Duchamp, anything can be art, there's a sense . . . in [the] poetry world—even within more innovative camps—that certain things are poetry and that certain things are not. Coming from the art world, this strikes me as an untenable & unsustainable stance, both aesthetically and historically and one that is bound to implode [at] any moment."

2

The conundrum of the nature of poetry is not a new confusion. To adapt queer theorist David Halperin's words to a completely different context, the definitional incoherence at the core of the modern notion of poetry is a sign of its historical evolution. These days, when we think of poetry, we think primarily of the lyric in its various permutations. Historically, however, different genres of poems have been recognized, each performing a different function. Beginning with the classical triad of lyric, narrative or epic, and dramatic poetry, these types have proliferated over the ages into lyric poems, narrative poems, epic poems, philosophical poems, didactic poems, satirical poems, meditative poems, elegies, etc. The categories often overlap, but one would not fault a satirical poem for being insufficiently elegiac.

To take only classical examples, *The Iliad* (an epic narrative), the Homeric Hymns, Pindar's panegyrics to the winners of athletic competitions, Sappho's love lyrics, and Lucretius's *De rerum natura* ("The Nature of Things," a didactic treatise on the nature of the physical and metaphysical universe) don't operate by the same principles. The range of possible poems has increased exponentially since then. As poet-blogger Gary Sullivan points out, "Poetry is not a single species. . . . [It] has an incredible number of not just forms (sonnet, pantoum, villanelle, sestina), but whole systems of values and concerns. There is language-centered writing, visual poetry (or 'vispo'), confessional poetry, flarf, procedural poetry, surrealism, lyrical poetry, epic poetry, spoken word, and so on."

In sharp contrast to such a capacious conception of poetry is talk-poet David Antin's famous assertion that "if Robert Lowell is a poet then I don't want to be a poet," not to mention the at-least-two-centuries-old quest among Western poets to find or define the distinction between poetry and prose, to achieve the zero degree of difference between poetry and prose by means of, most prominently, the prose poem, but also the abandonment of such markers of the "poetic" as rhyme, meter, figurative language, and the foregrounding of the poem's aural and oral elements.

In critic Virginia Jackson's words, "The notion that poetry is or ever was one genre is the primary symptom of the lyricization of poetry [the historical transformation of many varied poetic genres into the single abstraction of the post-Romantic lyric]: the songs, riddles, epigrams, sonnets, epitaphs, *blazons,* lieder, elegies, marches, dialogues, conceits, ballads, epistles, hymns, odes, eclogues, and monodramas considered lyric in the Western tradition before the early nineteenth century were not lyric in the same sense as the poetry that we think of as lyric. The fact that we think of almost all poetry as lyric is the secondary symptom of lyricization. When the stipulative functions of particular genres are collapsed into one big idea of poems as lyrics, then the only function poems can perform in our culture is to become individual or communal ideals. Such ideals might bind particular groups or sub-cultures (in slams, for example, or avant-garde blogs, or poetry cafés, or salons, or university, library, and museum reading series [not to mention some of the poetic movements Sullivan mentions above]), but the more ideally lyric poems and poetry culture have become, the fewer actual poetic genres address readers in specific ways. That ratio is responsible for our twenty-first-century sense that poetry is all-important and at the same time already in its afterlife" (183).

The word "lyric" derives from the word "lyre." Originally a lyric was a poem written to be sung, often to musical accompaniment (this sense is preserved in the use of the word "lyrics" to refer to the words of a song). Lyric has traditionally been defined by its foregrounding of the musical elements deriving from its origin (rhythmic and sonic patterning), though often the concept of "music" is metaphorical. Now the category of lyric has become a catchall or grab bag for any poem that is not explicitly and exclusively narrative or didactic, or perhaps satirical (humor tends to be excluded from most definitions of the lyric, though irony, subtler and better behaved, is welcome). *The New Princeton Encyclopedia of Poetry and Poetics* entry on "Lyric" points out that "much of the confusion in the modern critical usage of 'lyric' (i.e. usage after 1550) is due to an overextension of the term to cover a body of poetic writing that has radically altered its nature over the centuries of its development" (714).

"Lyric" uncomfortably accommodates a disparate and often contradictory array of kinds of poems. As *The New Princeton Encyclopedia of Poetry and Poetics* puts it, "In contemporary critical usage it may be said that 'lyric' is a general, categorical, and nominal term, whereas in the pre-Renaissance sense it was specific, generic, and descriptive" (715). Lyric has tended to slip from a description of a kind of poetry to a prescription for what poetry should be.

3

This piece was originally titled "There's No Such Thing as Poetry," a deliberately provocative title. Poet and critic Joan Houlihan asked whether I would still believe that statement if I substituted the word "writing" for the word "poetry." If one simply means putting symbolic marks on a surface with the intent of communicating something to someone, if only to oneself, or simply of recording something, then certainly there is such a thing as writing. It's a material and social practice, and readily identifiable. If one means something more second-order than that, by which some things would qualify as "writing" and some things wouldn't, moving from description to prescription, things get much more complicated.

Given the enormous range of things that can come under the heading of "writing," from grocery lists to love letters to newspaper articles to poems to scientific treatises to street signs to warning labels, one could realistically say that there's no such thing as writing, even more so than one could say for poetry. It doesn't follow from that premise that there's no such thing as good or bad writing. One would just have to define that in terms of the function of each kind of writing. Good writing for a nutritional label on a box of breakfast cereal is going to be rather different from good writing for a political speech or for a romance novel.

Any kind of writing can be well or badly written, more or less clear and accurate. Grammatical and factual accuracy, for example, is necessary to any good or effective writing, writing that successfully achieves its aims (though factual accuracy may be counter-indicated if one's intention with a piece of writing is to deceive). Beyond this foundation of communicating accurately on the literal level (making sense in the most basic sense), the different genres of writing, from street signs to poems to instruction manuals to press releases, have different standards of evaluation, depending on their intentions and their uses. As Steven Pinker points out in a discussion of metaphor, "Multiple, partial, and emotionally charged similarities add to the richness of poetry, but they detract from understanding in science" (264). The very ambiguity that renders an instruction manual useless can be the thing we value in a poem, opening it up to multiple interpretations. When you're trying to put together a grill from a set of instructions, semantic polyvalence is the last thing you want to encounter; but in a poem, you may find its absence a flaw, rendering the poem too flat and literal.

4

It would make things more clear, and eliminate much controversy and polemic, if we acknowledged that poetry isn't a singular thing, that there are different kinds of poetry, and that these different kinds have different aims, different audiences, and different effects. Let's see them for the distinct things they are and the distinct things they do. Sometimes one wants to be challenged. At other times one wants to be entertained, or soothed when one is stressed, or comforted when one is sad. Sometimes one wants to discover something new; sometimes one seeks familiarity. There's no reason to think that poems should fulfill all these different needs, or that they should be expected to do so. On the other hand, there's no reason to think that there aren't legitimately different kinds of poems that differently address different readers' needs and desires, or even the same reader's different needs at different times and in different moods. To refer to another mode of artistic experience, sometimes I want to listen to Wagner and sometimes I want to listen to Webern (to take two extremes of scale); sometimes I want to listen to Joy Division and sometimes I want to listen to Kylie Minogue. No one wants to be challenged all the time. But no one wants to chuckle or be sung to sleep all the time either.

The vast majority of poetry out there doesn't interest me. Much of it I actively dislike. But except in my grumpier moods, I don't begrudge it its right to exist in its own spheres. I just don't want to read it. I don't object to the Rod McKuens and Matty J. Stepaneks of the world. In high school I was very taken with Hugh Prather's New Age prattling, which I found in the poetry section of the Macon Mall's Waldenbooks. I don't even mind if Jewel and Ashanti and T-Boz want to write poetry, though it would be nice if Jewel knew what the word "casualty" meant. I had never heard of Jack Prelutsky, whom the Poetry Foundation named as America's first Children's Poet Laureate, but his rhymes about tomatoes and asparaguses seem harmless enough, and even somewhat amusing. Such work might as well exist on other planets; those worlds don't impinge on mine.

It angers me when work that I care for is weighed and found wanting not because it fails to live up to its aims but because it doesn't offer the comforting homilies of the *Prairie Home Companion* (which to be fair does sometimes feature interesting poems) or the narrowly defined entertainment value poetic populists demand. It angers me when "intellectual" is used as a pejorative. It angers me when such pseudo-populism is held up as a model of what all poetry should be for all people.

The complaints of those who bemoan contemporary poetry's difficulty and inaccessibility show a real lack of familiarity with contemporary poetry. They needn't like contemporary poetry, but they should at least describe it accurately. Eliot and Stevens, condemned by many then and now for their "intellectualism," have been dead for a long time. Except for the fact that they write in free verse, most contemporary American poets proceed as if Modernism never happened. Vernon Shetley, in his book *After the Death of Poetry: Poet and Audience in Contemporary America,* which argues that contemporary poetry needs to be more complex and challenging to capture and hold readers' interest, quotes Joseph Epstein's observation that "contemporary poetry has not grown more but less difficult" (3). The Ron Sillimans and Clark Coolidges of the poetry world(s) are far outnumbered by the legions of competent poets writing completely accessible poems about their divorces and their dying grandmothers.

The grumblings of those who bemoan contemporary poetry's elitism and inaccessibility remind me of the readers Howard Nemerov wrote of many years ago: "They don't like poetry, even though some of them feel they ought to; and they very naturally want poems to be as easy as possible, in order that there may be no intellectual embarrassment about despising them. These readers get their entire pleasure, not from reading poems, but from wrangling interminably over 'communication,' as though each of them lived in his own telephone booth" ("The Difficulty of Difficult Poetry," *Reflexions* 24).

The problem, in poetry as in our culture in general, is of leveling. Everything is brought down to the lowest common denominator. Some years ago, when I lived in Chicago, I attended a screening of a film biography of the late Martinican Négritude poet Aimé Césaire, a fascinating and challenging poet who also had a rather interesting life. During the question and answer period someone asked, "What does this film have to say to the average black kid on the street corner?" I wondered, "Why does it have to speak to him? Isn't there enough in our culture that's addressed to him, that panders, however patronizingly and exploitatively, to him?" And isn't it insulting to assume that he couldn't find something interesting and engaging in Césaire if he were given the chance to do so? To assume that the mythical "average person" can't appreciate anything complex is rank condescension. But in our culture, anything "intellectual," anything complex or difficult, is not only marginalized but dismissed as irrelevant or, most damningly, "elitist," often by members of the socio-economic elite.

5

All good writing, from a political speech to a love letter to a philosophical disquisition to a detective thriller to, yes, even a poem, shares grammatical fluency (one must know the rules of syntax to break them effectively), lexical accuracy (one must know a word's meaning in order to play with or revise it), particularity and specificity of diction, phrasing, and imagery, and an avoidance of cliché and vagueness. What may work for a song lyric or spoken word poem will probably not work for a poem on the page, bereft of the musical texture, the grain of the performer's voice, the gestures of performance. But with regard to particularity and some degree of uniqueness, good song lyrics are not different from good poems for the page.

Within the very broad and capacious limits of what might be called good writing, I say let a hundred flowers bloom. That emphatically includes the more exotic and recherché, even the off-putting. Not all flowers are beautiful, and not all smell lovely. (Philosopher and art critic Arthur C. Danto has pointed out that some art isn't meant to be beautiful, and even that some art, given the effect it aims for, shouldn't be beautiful.) Let there be room for that which doesn't appeal to the widest possible audience and doesn't intend to. I have as much a right to my aesthetic pleasures (and challenges: I enjoy reading poetry, but pleasure isn't the only reason for reading) as Ted Kooser or Dana Gioia does. I refuse to submit poetry, or life in general, to the tyranny of the majority. There are worse things than being unpopular, and just because you're outnumbered doesn't mean that you're wrong.

As a corrective to prevalent misunderstandings and misuses of the term and the idea, anthropologist Marshall Sahlins offers the following clarification: "Cultural relativism is first and last an interpretive [methodological] procedure. It is not the moral argument that any culture or custom is as good as any other, if not better. Relativism is the simple prescription that, in order to be intelligible, other people's practices and ideals must be placed in their own historical context, understood as positional values in the field of their own cultural relationships rather than appreciated by categorical and moral judgments of our own making. Relativity is the provisional suspension of one's own judgments in order to situate the practices at issue in the historical and cultural order that made them possible. It is in no other way a matter of advocacy" (46).

Just as anthropologists have recognized that there is no such singular and universal thing as "culture," we in the literary world should acknowledge that there is no such unitary thing as "poetry." I call for a poetic relativism modeled on Marshall Sahlins's definition of cultural relativism, which doesn't exclude judgment, but postpones such judgment until the poem has been understood on its own terms. It is only then that one can determine one's position toward those terms, to evaluate whether what was done was done well or badly, and to decide whether it was worth doing at all. Joan Houlihan cogently points out that letting all flowers bloom doesn't preclude the possibility or even the necessity of weeding once they've done so, though this would hardly be the wholesale mowing-down (of poems or of poets) that the allusion to Mao might imply.

WORKS CITED

Jackson, Virginia. "Who Reads Poetry?" *PMLA* 13.1, January 2008.

Nemerov, Howard. *Reflexions on Poetry and Poetics.* New Brunswick: Rutgers University Press, 1972.

The New Princeton Encyclopedia of Poetry and Poetics. Ed. Alex Preminger and T. V. F. Brogan. Princeton: Princeton University Press, 1993.

Pinker, Steven. *The Stuff of Thought.* New York: Viking, 2007.

Sahlins, Marshall. *Waiting for Foucault, Still.* Chicago: Prickly Paradigm Press, 2002.

Shetley, Vernon. *After the Death of Poetry: Poet and Audience in Contemporary America.* Durham: Duke University Press, 1993.

How Do You Mean That?

Some Thoughts on Meaning in Poems

1

What kinds of meanings do poems present to us? What does meaning mean? (There are two ways to read that question.) In the entry "Meaning, Problem of" (whose title is almost a poem in itself) in the (old) *Princeton Encyclopedia of Poetry and Poetics,* author Murray Krieger writes that "especially worrisome is the use of this word in reference to the peculiar kind of symbols employed in poetic discourse. For purposes of economy we shall simply restrict 'meaning' to its primitive sense which concerns the reference of verbal symbols and their syntactic relations to the outside world of things and their real relations. This limitation will immediately dismiss that perhaps eccentric sense of 'meaning,' in somewhat common usage of late in poetics, which would treat only the aesthetic, intramural coherence among the words of a literary work in accordance with the internal consistency of their closed system of interrelations" (476). With the exception of that "only," it is exactly this "perhaps eccentric" sense that interests me. It may be just as well that Krieger dismisses it: that leaves me free to discourse upon, around, and beside it.

In his poem "Ars Poetica," Archibald MacLeish famously wrote, in lines that violate their own dictum, "A poem should not mean / But be." I would amend that to say that a poem should mean by being, that it should be an embodiment and not just the vehicle of meaning. Being and embodiment are kinds of meaning. We are each alive on this earth, after all, and what do I mean, what do you mean? We mean ourselves and everything that we are. Similarly, the poem means itself, though as an object and event in the world it can incorporate and respond to other objects and events in the world (nothing exists in isolation). MacLeish also wrote that "A poem should be palpable and mute / As a globed fruit." That bodily quality is something I look for in others' poems and strive for in my own.

As T. S. Eliot writes, "poetry is a form of 'communication,' yet that which is to be communicated is the poem itself, and only incidentally the experience and the thought which have gone into it" ("The Use of Poetry and the Use of Criticism," *Selected Prose* 80). The poem "has a reality which is not simply the reality of what the writer is trying to 'express,' or of his experience of writing it, or of the experience of the reader or of the writer as reader. Consequently the problem of what a poem 'means' is a good deal more difficult than it at first appears" ("Use of Poetry").

In this regard I am at least partially an heir to the Romantic poetics of Coleridge (though without his confidence that the real and its figures can "exactly coincide"), as opposed to or at least distinct from the mimetic aesthetics of Plato and Sir Philip Sidney: for me, meaning in poems is organic, not propositional. I am an adherent of the idea of what Cleanth Brooks called "presentational meaning": the poem is an experience in itself, not a statement about experience (though statements can certainly be part of the experience that is the poem). "Meaning in this sense of the term is made up, mediately or immediately, of all that appears, no matter how great or small its importance" (Adorno 218).

In his "Adagia," Wallace Stevens writes that "there is no wing like meaning" (*Collected Poetry and Prose* 903). While this proposes that meaning is incommensurable, it also posits meaning not as an end but as a means: a wing is something with which one travels, which takes one somewhere else. Given that poems are so often seen as vessels of meaning, it's interesting that this aphorism makes meaning the vehicle, not the destination.

In "The Use of Poetry and the Use of Criticism," T. S. Eliot goes even further, writing that "the chief use of the 'meaning' of a poem, in the ordinary sense, may be (for I am speaking of some kinds of poetry and not all) to satisfy one habit of the reader, to keep his mind diverted and quiet, while the poem does its work upon him: much as the imaginary burglar is always provided with a bit of nice meat for the house-dog. This is a normal situation of which I approve. But the minds of all poets do not work that way; some of them, assuming that there are other minds like their own, become impatient of this 'meaning' which seems superfluous, and perceive possibilities of intensity through its elimination. . . . A great deal, in the way of meaning, belongs to prose rather than to poetry" (93). I don't think that it's as easy to eliminate meaning as Eliot implies. It's in our nature to invest objects and events with meaning, especially human products, all of which are suffused with human intention. We cannot look with a disinterested cold eye on anything humans have made. As Adorno reminds us, "Art continues to live up to the postulate of meaning even though it rigorously negates it" (221). It's the nature of that meaning that interests me.

2

Someone recently asked me what one of my poems meant, and I realized that I had never thought about it. I rarely think about what my poems mean, though I often wish to get at something in and with them, to do something by means of them. But that something is part of the experience of the poem, not a gloss on or an explanation of it.

When I am writing a poem, I think about the clarity of the images and the precision and accuracy of the phrasing. I think about the music of words in relation and the rhythms of the phrases, the aural shape of the poem as a whole. I think about the feeling I want the poem to embody, or the feeling that the poem wants to embody. But I rarely think about a paraphrasable meaning, of how I would explicate the poem.

"What an artist has to say is said through figuration; it is never a message carried by figuration" (Adorno 216). T. S. Eliot was once asked what he meant by the line "Lady, three white leopards sat under a juniper tree," from "Ash Wednesday," to which he replied, "I meant, 'Lady, three white leopards sat under a juniper tree.'" While he was doubtlessly being a bit recalcitrant, he was emphasizing that a poem's meaning isn't under or over or even inside its words. It is those words, and the experience of reading them. There are three white leopards under a juniper tree, or at least their verbal simulacrum. If Eliot had wanted you to see or imagine something else, he would have written something else. Even if those leopards are symbolic, they must first be themselves before they can stand in for anything else. To adapt Hugh Kenner's words to a quite different sense, "Has anyone . . . ever suspected how many lines of *Ash-Wednesday* [*sic*] simply meant what they said? . . . Nothing is so unbelievable as exact truth told in a calm voice" (277).

While I don't often think about what a poem, either my own or someone else's, means, I do think about what's happening in the poem. Terry Eagleton has written that Eliot wasn't concerned with what a poem said, but with what it did. And W. H. Auden called poetry a way of happening.

My poems aren't puzzles to be solved; they don't have hidden meanings waiting to be uncovered. If a poem is conceived of as a puzzle or a riddle, then once you've discovered the key, once you've worked out the puzzle, you're finished with the poem and can get on with your life. That's not how I approach poems. Perhaps because so many poets, and almost all literary critics, teach, spending their days explaining things, we too often approach poems as problems to be figured out, rather than as experiences to be explored and enjoyed. Pleasure is often left out of consideration, if not actively denigrated. Charles Bernstein, for example, seems to distrust pleasure; his notion of the anti-absorptive seems like a prophylactic to ward off the possibility of being taken in or seduced, of succumbing to the opiate of the literary masses. In this regard what might be called literary leftists resemble too many political leftists: pleasure is regarded with suspicion, and life is just a set of necessary tasks. I once shared a panel on difficulty in poetry with Robert Collins, co-editor of *The Birmingham Poetry Review*, on which he pointed out that, though Horace said that poetry should instruct and delight, much experimental poetry insists on instruction to the detriment of delight. I read poems because I like them, not because they're good for me, though they might well be. If a poem doesn't give pleasure on a certain level, including the pleasure of being engagingly challenged and surprised, then who cares what it means?

Sometimes when reading a poem I'll wonder about a line or a phrase, "What the hell does this mean?" (What gives me the most trouble is syntactical difficulty: if I can't follow the syntax, can't make sense of the words' relations to one another, I'm lost.) But that's usually on the level of literal statement—"What's being said?"—not the level of interpretation—"What's the significance of what's being said?" Explicative and interpretative difficulty are often conflated or confused. When we speak of the meaning of a poem or any utterance, we can be referring to two different things: the literal sense, and the way in which that utterance is intended to be taken. It's important to be clear about which is which in any given case. If one asks someone about a statement of theirs, "What do you mean by that?" it's not usually because one doesn't understand what was said, but because one doesn't understand its significance, one doesn't know *why* it was said.

Poems frame utterances, including utterances that could never be spoken by any plausible or even any imaginable speaker, thus imbuing them with significance. But the significance of an utterance may well be that it's in a poem, that it's a piece of language to which we've been asked to pay attention, to notice in the way that we don't usually have the time or inclination to do in our everyday lives: in William Carlos Williams's words, "This is just to say." In his book *Semiotics of Poetry,* Michael Riffaterre points out that "literary description only apparently returns us to things, to signifieds; poetic representation is founded on a reference to the signifiers" (198), though I think that Riffaterre, like many others, neglects the extent to which words are things in themselves, and not just signifiers of things. Poems ask us to see them as and for themselves, to see their language as not just expression or communication but as event and object: in James Longenbach's words, "A poem might feel more like a concatenation of various linguistic strands than like the utterance of a single person" (14)—or, I would add, even like the utterances of several persons. Poems ask us to see them as and for themselves, to see their language as not just expression or communication but as event and object. Meaning is never absent, but meaning isn't the meaning of the poem. As Hart Crane describes his goal in "General Aims and Theories," "It is as if the poem gave the reader as he left it a single, new word, never before spoken and impossible to actually enunciate, but self-evident as an active principle in the reader's consciousness henceforward" (Gioa et al. 126).

WORKS CITED

Adorno, Theodor. *Aesthetic Theory.* Trans. C. Lenhardt. New York: Routledge and Kegan Paul, 1984.

Eliot, T. S. *Selected Prose of T. S. Eliot.* Ed. Frank Kermode. New York: Farrar, Straus and Giroux, 1975.

Gioia, Dana, et al., eds. *Twentieth Century American Poetics: Poets on the Art of Poetry.* New York: McGraw Hill, 2003.

Kenner, Hugh. *The Pound Era.* Berkeley: University of California Press, 1973.

Krieger, Murray. "Meaning, Problem Of." *Princeton Encyclopedia of Poetry and Poetics.* Ed. Alex Preminger, Frank J. Warnke, and O. B. Hardison Jr. Princeton: Princeton University Press, 1965.

Longenbach, James. *The Art of the Poetic Line.* St. Paul: Graywolf Press, 2007.

Riffaterre, Michael. *Semiotics of Poetry.* Bloomington: Indiana University Press, 1978.

Stevens, Wallace. *Collected Poetry and Prose.* Ed. Frank Kermode and Joan Richardson. New York: The Library of America, 1997.

Picture This

On the Concept of Poetic Imagery

1

A teacher I had in high school said once, "Images are a dime a dozen. I'm tired of them." A professor in college warned, "Don't let metaphors become pets." Some years later, one of my own students told me, "I don't want to look at pictures when I'm reading a poem." The still predominant scenic mode, to use Charles Altieri's term, is so heavily dependent on imagery and visual description that it's become completely rote. If I've painted a verbal picture, I've written a poem. It sometimes seems that anyone can come up with a string of images. It's the structure that's hard to produce, some reason that these particular images appear together in this particular order or constellation. Of course, it's sadly impressive how many writers can't even come up with disconnected images of any precision or impact. But while I'm critical of the scenic mode, I'm quite wedded to images, and to the specificity and groundedness images can provide. I don't like to float off into the ether, and imagery can provide ballast, a route from here to there, wherever "there" may be for any given poem. Vivid, striking images make a strong impression on me, and I strive for them in my own work as part of the sensuous experience of the poem. All good poems, of whatever mode or style, have in common specificity and particularity. In contemporary American poetry, that specificity is primarily imagistic.

What we mean when we talk about images in poetry are mental images. A mental image can be defined as "the connecting link between experience (object) and knowledge (subject). An image [is] the reproduction in the mind of a sensation produced in perception. . . . But of course the mind may also produce images when not receiving direct perceptions," as in remembering past events or objects no longer present, in dreams, or in reading, where words "may refer either to experiences which could produce physical perceptions were the reader actually to have those experiences, or to the sense-impressions themselves" ("Imagery," *New Princeton Encyclopedia* 559, 560). While the words "image" and "imagery" have been used in many and various senses in literary criticism, it is in this basic sense that I use them here.

In his *ABC of Reading*, Ezra Pound writes of three ways that language can be charged with meaning, which he calls phanopoeia, melopoeia, and logopoeia. He defines phanopoeia as "throwing the object (fixed or moving) on to the visual imagination," much like projecting an image onto a screen (63). The reader's imagination is presumably the screen which passively accepts this image. (This is a problematic view of the reading process, discounting the reader's active role in producing the text, but I will leave that discussion for a later time.) Pound emphasizes that phanopoeia includes not just the fixed, still image but the moving image, that is, "praxis or action" (52). Most imagery in contemporary American poetry, as in Imagism, is of the fixed, still variety. (For Pound, at least for a time, vorticism was the solution to this problem of stasis.) Melopoeia induces "emotional correlations by the sound and rhythm of the speech" (63). Pound describes, in turn, three kinds of melopoeia, "verse made to sing; to chant or intone; and to speak" (61), and recommends the first. Louis Zukofsky followed this line of thinking with his diagram of poetry as "upper limit music, lower limit speech." Pound's definition of logopoeia is the most problematic of the three. Logopoeia induces "both of the effects by stimulating the associations (intellectual or emotional) that have remained in the reader's consciousness in relation to the actual words or word groups employed" (63). It's unclear to me what the two effects are meant to be. It seems that they are visual imagery and emotional associations, but since the effects are induced by the stimulation of intellectual or emotional effects, that doesn't seem possible, unless Pound is saying that emotional associations are induced by the stimulation of emotional associations, which is completely circular.

In the interest of clarity and at the risk of distortion, I define phanopoeia as the deployment of imagery to produce an effect upon the reader; melopoeia as the use of the range of verbal music toward this aim; and logopoeia as a second-order technique, using ideas, connotations, and intellectual and emotional associations to produce an effect in the reader. In Pound's terms, logopoeia may be referred to as the poetry of the ideas, as distinct from the poetry of the words (melopoeia) or, to add a category Pound does not write of, the poetry of the images (phanopoeia).

Not all imagery is visual. Norman Friedman's *New Princeton Encyclopedia of Poetry and Poetics* entry on "Imagery" lists a whole panoply of kinds of mental imagery: "visual (sight, then brightness, clarity, color, and motion), auditory (hearing), olfactory (smell), gustatory (taste), tactile (touch, then temperature, texture), organic (awareness of heartbeat, pulse, breathing, digestion), and kinesthetic (awareness of muscle tension and movement)" (560). It also points out that different poets may use different kinds of imagery, arguing that Keats's poetry is dominated by tactile and organic imagery and Shelley's by kinesthetic imagery. At the risk of simplifying a complex topic, I concentrate here on visual imagery, as most imagery in contemporary American poetry is of the visual kind.

Much contemporary American poetry neglects melopoeia, the music of syllables and words and phrases, in favor of phanopoeia, the play of imagery, or in the case of avant-garde poetry, some of which reads like a "Cliff's Notes" version of theory, logopoeia, the play of ideas. Too often, however, the images neither play nor work, and the ideas are out on strike. (Horace wrote that poetry should instruct and delight, but too much contemporary poetry skimps on the delight and teaches nothing one didn't already know.)

2

I've become interested in what I call the image-phrase, which isn't strictly descriptive or visual but evocative or connotative (something along the lines of the absent presence of a flower that has never existed conjured up by the word *fleur* for Mallarmé). It's a kind of conceptual abstraction of the image that conjures up the visual without attempting to paint a picture. The image-phrase strikes me as a more flexible concept than the image per se. The image-phrase mingles perception and conception; it captures the inseparability of image and language, and also the way that a phrase can produce an image that is not a picture of something. The aim is a perhaps paradoxical sharp-edged, precise evocation.

Words are not pictorial, except in their visual presence as marks on a surface, a presence which is in itself not linguistic. There are no images in poems. There are conjunctions of words by means of which the poet hopes to induce the reader to produce a mental image in his or her mind (and such an "image" is as much verbal as visual), an image that will be analogous to the image the poet wants to appear at that point in the poem. "As far as poetry is concerned, there are no sensuous visions that correspond to what a poem tries to say. Instead, . . . the concrete actualization of poetry lies in its linguistic shape, not in the highly problematic visual representations poems are supposed to stimulate. Poems do not need sensual representation to actualize themselves. They are concrete enough in the medium of language" (Adorno 143–44). In Saussurean terms, one presents the signifier rather than the referent, which is always unattainable in any case: the concept rather than the thing in the world.

Jack Spicer writes in one of his letters "to" Lorca that he tried to be "independent of images . . . to make things visible rather than to make pictures of them" (*After Lorca,* Spicer 34). This is close to what the image-phrase attempts to do, knowing that it is an impossible aim. Spicer, though, claims to seek "to make poems out of real objects," though he also claims, contradictorily, that he wants "to point to the real" (33), which would indicate that those objects have stubbornly stayed outside the poem. An object in a poem, unlike the strips of newspaper and wallpaper pasted into Picasso's collage painting *Glass and Bottle of Suze,* is not a real object, but a virtual object, a verbal simulacrum of objecthood. A poem cannot be constructed out of things, or even ideas and emotions. As Mallarmé reportedly told Degas, poems are not made out of ideas, but out of words. The only objects in poems are words, and words are not objects in the same way that globs of paint, that shapes and colors, are.

Words can elicit visual responses in the reader's mind (though the relationship between a reader's visual response and the visual impression aimed at by the poem is contingent at best), but the paradox of how a visual impression or experience is conveyed or re-created in a nonvisual medium is irresolvable. Much as we might wish them to, words do not embody things. How often I've been frustrated by language's incapacity to capture a visual impression, the nearly-full moon at eight haloed by a pink-tinged mist and wreathed by a half-circle of bare and partly-bare branches black against the blue-fading-into-deeper-blue night. So many words and that moon's still not there. As W. J. T. Mitchell points out, "Since literary representation does not represent by likeness the way pictorial images do, literary representation is itself only and always metaphorical" ("Image," *New Princeton Encyclopedia* 557). The idea of representation is a metaphor when applied to literature. Visual images bear a perceptual resemblance to the things that they represent, but words do not resemble that which they attempt to represent, except insofar as they represent other words (as in literary presentations of speech, writing, or verbal thought). Verbal descriptions are never depictions. "The concept of 'poetic imagery' is thus a kind of oxymoron, installing an alien medium (painting, sculpture, visual art) at the heart of verbal expression" ("Image" 557).

3

Painting and writing work very differently in this regard, because a painting is always itself an image, even if it's not an image of anything. There are actual colors and actual shapes that, whether or not they refer to something else, exist as material entities in themselves. A painting, or a sculpture, can be thought of as an image of itself. I often prefer nonrepresentational art exactly for this reason. Representational paintings seem on the one hand redundant (an image that's also imaging something else) and on the other hand distracting (the image being represented takes one's attention away from the image the painting is: and I'm very easily distracted by subject matter). I've seen the world, and I don't particularly need copies of it. My interest is in the painting as a painting, not as a painting of something. As Adorno writes of traditionally representational paintings, "To the extent to which we detect in them images rather than replicas of something, they are 'abstract'" (46).

Clyfford Still's wholly abstract paintings are landscapes of color and shape. There's a large all-black painting of his at the Art Institute of Chicago (I can't recall the title, though I've tried to look it up) that's like a sea of black with black islands of textured paint rising out of the surface. How often I've been tempted to touch that painting, to feel the textures that the eye only intuits. But words, as words, don't have that palpable solidity, that visceral immediacy. We hear or we read and we must then translate.

Language is an in-betweenness, the interrelation of elements. Language doesn't just relate things: language is relation. If it's purely material, it's no longer language, just scrawlings or noise (though it might then become visual art, like the work of Cy Twombly or Arakawa, or music, like some of Karlheinz Stockhausen's language experiments). If it's purely conceptual, without manifestation, then it's no longer language either. Some experimental poetry (concrete poetry, for example; I don't know what the poetic equivalent of conceptual art would be) tries to approach one or the other of those extremes as closely as possible while still remaining language.

The sound of a word can fill the mouth or ear with pleasure, but that sound isn't the word. A beautifully scripted or typeset word can give visual pleasure, but those marks on the page aren't the word either. Nor is the verbal concept in the mind, unspoken. Words are defined by their liminal state between the immaterial and two states of concretion, thoughts on the one hand and marks or sounds on the other. It's the conjunction and co-presence of these two modes that makes language language.

WORKS CITED

Adorno, Theodor. *Aesthetic Theory.* Trans. C. Lenhardt. New York: Routledge and Kegan Paul, 1984.

The New Princeton Encyclopedia of Poetry and Poetics. Ed. Alex Preminger and T. V. F. Brogan. Princeton: Princeton University Press, 1993.

Pound, Ezra. *ABC of Reading.* New York: New Direction, 1960.

Spicer, Jack. *After Lorca.* In The *Collected Books of Jack Spicer.* Ed. Robin Blaser. Los Angeles: Black Sparrow Press, 1975.

On Difficulty in Poetry

What are these songs
straining at sense—
you the consequence?
—Louis Zukofsky, "Anew 10"

1

It's been the fashion at least since the Modernists to complain that contemporary poetry has become difficult, and that this difficulty has alienated the readers who used to flock to poetry as they now flock to John Grisham novels and *American Idol.* I am not sure what constitutes the easy poetry these people look back to: Shakespeare? Donne? Milton? I'm also not sure when and where this massive poetry audience existed. The great majority of the nineteenth-century counterparts of those who now watch television and read pulp fiction were barely literate. They certainly weren't seduced away from their immersion in Keats and Browning by the advent of the mass media. Conversely, Dylan Thomas was one of the most popular poets of the 1940s and '50s, on both sides of the Atlantic, and his work is nothing if not "difficult" (and it isn't nothing, though it is somewhat forgotten today). And both avant-gardeners and poetic populists are often too busy bashing T. S. Eliot to remember that he practically filled arenas when he gave readings. Today John Ashbery and Jorie Graham, whose work is usually considered to be challenging at the least, are among our most popular poets, prominent enough to have each been profiled in *The New Yorker,* a magazine not usually known for overly taxing its readers.

I don't believe that the imaginary "average person" doesn't want to be challenged and stimulated. There is, for example, a whole industry of verbal challenges, from crossword puzzles to Scrabble, that the so-called general public relishes.

In the perennially popular "death of poetry" discourse, there's a consensus that people don't read poetry because it's too hard, too "elitist" (another word that should be expunged from the English language: it's never descriptive, only pejorative). I've always thought the opposite, that most poetry isn't hard enough, in the sense that's it's not interesting or engaging enough. It doesn't hold the attention—you read it once or twice and you've used it up. That engagement I look for and too often miss is a kind of pleasure, in the words, the rhythms, the palpable texture of the poem. It's the opposite of boredom.

Literary critic Vernon Shetley, who observes that most contemporary poetry has grown less, not more difficult, since the Moderns (perhaps it might be more accurate to say, most contemporary "mainstream" poetry), argues in his book *After the Death of Poetry: Poet and Audience in Contemporary America* that "only by increasing the level of intellectual challenge it offers can poetry once again make itself a vital part of intellectual culture" (3–4). I would add that poetry's challenges and pleasures are far more diverse than the intellectual, though I do believe that the intellectual is an essential element in poetry: to modify Eliot's dictum, the poem must be as intelligent as possible.

Many years ago I sat in on a class of Ted Kooser's in which he asserted that a reader wants to be led by the hand through a poem, that readers have no patience with being baffled, no tolerance for mystery. I had to interject that I hated to be led by the hand through a poem. I'd rather that the poet assume that I can make my own way through a poem, though I do prefer that there at least be pathways, even if they're not paved and lit. I don't object to being baffled, though I may not wish to remain in bafflement indefinitely. Just as mystery can be part of a person's allure, so mystery in poetry can be a lure. Yeats calls this "the fascination of what's difficult." One wants to solve the mystery, or at least better understand its source. Sometimes one discovers that the mystery isn't to be solved, but still that process of exploration has helped one to know it better, to experience it more fully. (Superficial mystery is merely shallowness posing as depth. As Howard Nemerov notes, some poets "wish to make common matters singular, easy matters hard, and shallow thoughts profound.") To quote a perhaps unlikely source, Billy Collins has written that, "in the best of all possible worlds of reading, dealing with difficulty can be listed among poetry's pleasures" (25).

What I cannot bear, as a reader or as a person, is to be bored. For a poem to be boring is much worse than for a poem to be baffling. In Marianne Moore's words, "Paramount as a rule for any kind of writing—scientific, commercial, informal, prose or verse—we dare not be dull" ("Idiosyncrasy and Technique," *Marianne Moore Reader* 172). (Dullness is as much the enemy of poetry now as it was when Pope wrote.) Incomprehension and even frustration can seduce in poems just as they can in people: many objects of desire are obscure, but their outlines are clear. What does the sunlight breaking through the clouds that have hovered all day, then filtering through the leaves of the giant live oak tree in my back yard, "mean"? It is, I saw it, I felt in on my skin. You can see something too, feel that slight difference in the temperature when you step out from under that tree, your feet sinking a little into the thick layer of leaf litter. Too many bad poems, dull poems, are just meaning, with nothing or too little doing the meaning. I know what they mean, but I can't be bothered to care. As Charles Bernstein notes, some poems are easy because they have nothing to say. Conversely, some poems are difficult for the same reason, in an attempt to cover up their vacuity. Irish poet Mark Granier points out that some poems are difficult merely in the manner of a difficult child, sullenly or gleefully sticking out their tongues at the reader.

It's often said that "difficult" poems exclude potential readers. I feel excluded by poems that give me nothing to do as a reader, that offer me no new experience and nothing I didn't already know. It's wearying to read such poems, it makes me want to watch music videos instead, where at least one sometimes gets some glimpses of shirtless guys with six-pack abs. Any good poem gives the reader something, what Allen Grossman calls the interest of the world: feelings, sensations, experiences. T. S. Eliot wrote that genuine poetry can communicate before it's understood. I would say analogously that good poetry can and should give pleasure before it's understood. As Wallace Stevens noted of his supreme fiction, it must give pleasure. It's this pleasure that makes one want to understand the poem. Whether my poems are always immediately graspable in terms of subject matter, I've always tried to give the reader something, in terms of language, imagery, rhythm, etc., to make the poem a sensual experience. Understanding something can be a pleasurable experience (it can also be intensely painful), but in poetry as in life there are other pleasures than understanding. In Billy Collins's words, "Surely, you can enjoy a poem before you understand it. . . . The grasping of a poem's meaning, however provisional it may be, is only one of the many pleasures that poetry offers" (29).

I don't "understand" some of my favorite poems. I don't know what they "mean," but I know what happens to me when I read them; I know the experience I've had and its effect on me. Hart Crane has been one of my favorite poets for over twenty years, but until I taught him I didn't "understand" "The Broken Tower." I'm glad that I do now, but only because that understanding has enriched an experience I was already having.

Geoffrey Hill observes that "difficult poetry is the most democratic, because you are doing your audience the honour of supposing that they are intelligent human beings. If you write as if you had to placate or in any way entice their lack of interest, then I think you are making condescending assumptions about people. I mean people are not fools. But so much of the populist poetry of today treats people as if they were fools." I don't want to be patronized or condescended to, as a reader or a person; I would prefer that the poet assume that I am both intelligent and interested.

The ideal reader is on the one hand willing and alert enough to actively participate in the poem's production of meaning and on the other hand demanding enough to insist that the poem provide the material with which to produce such meaning and perceptive enough to see whether or not these pieces actually do form some kind of gestalt, however unexpected its shape. The poem may not adhere to standard, linear logic, but it must have a logic of its own.

2

It's always important to define one's terms, and yet it's rarely done. In order to clarify my topic, I offer here my anatomy of difficulty in poetry. I present the several kinds of difficulty in order of ascending complexity.

There is, first, lexical difficulty: the poem contains words with whose sense we are unfamiliar, or words used at variance from or even contrary to their dictionary definitions. Hart Crane's poetry is a perfect example of such difficulty, full of both arcane and recherché words ("infrangible," "transmemberment") and of words given idiosyncratic or private meanings: for example, the use of the word "calyx" to mean both a cornucopia (ironic, since the bounty is death's) and "the vortex made by a sinking vessel" (Crane's explication) in this stanza from "At Melville's Tomb":

> And wrecks passed without sound of bells,
> The calyx of death's bounty giving back
> A scattered chapter, livid hieroglyph,
> The portent wound in corridors of shells.

Then there is allusive difficulty; the poem that alludes frequently eludes. The poet refers to something we've not heard of, assumes a piece of knowledge we don't have. If one doesn't know that Herman Melville wrote obsessively about the sea, then one won't understand that the ocean itself is treated as his final resting place, though the man himself died on dry land. If one does not have "But at my back I always hear / Time's wingèd chariot hurrying near," and the rest of "To His Coy Mistress," in one's ear, the relationship of poem and title of Archibald MacLeish's "You, Andrew Marvell" will appear rather opaque, and some of the poem's sense of doom may be lost. Similarly, if one does not recognize the place names ("And Lebanon fade out and Crete / High through the clouds and overblown // And over Sicily the air / Still flashing"), one will miss the grim irony of darkness flooding in from the east, usually associated with sunrise, rather than from the west. Sometimes the allusion is implicit or indirect: one will miss some of the force (and some of the humor) of Frost's "For Once, Then, Something," if one misses the presence of Narcissus in love with his own image in a pool in its description of a man who sees "Me myself in the summer heaven" reflected in the water of a well. In this case, one must not only recognize the allusion, but notice that an allusion is being made at all. Poems considered difficult often allude to material outside the common literary or intellectual frame of reference. Modernist poetry is particularly difficult in its wide range and idiosyncratic, often inexplicit, deployment of allusion.

There is also syntactical difficulty, the obstacle of complex, unfamiliar, dislocated, broken, or incomplete syntax: one cannot discern or reconstruct the relations of the grammatical units. Swerving away from the conventions of prose syntax has long been an integral part of poetic practice: as Howard Nemerov explains, it is "precisely the sort of rhetorical and musical variation which properly belongs to poetry and distinguishes it from prose" ("The Difficulty of Difficult Poetry," *Reflexions* 25). The long, Latinate sentences of Milton's *Paradise Lost* are one example of this kind of difficulty; the fragmented, fractured syntax of much experimental poetry is another. In the case of *Paradise Lost,* one can parse the syntax with patience and careful attention; in many avant-garde poems, the syntax is intended to remain indeterminate, deliberately unparsable, resisting the reader's desire to make it cohere. It sometimes seems that the main mark of an "avant-garde" poem is the replacement of hypotaxis by parataxis, the substitution of the sentence fragment for complex or complete syntax.

There is also the case of semantic difficulty: we have trouble determining or deciding what a poem says or means, we cannot immediately decipher or interpret it. (It is important here to remember that sense and reference are distinct: sense is internal to the poem, as it is to language itself. As linguist David Crystal elucidates in *How Language Works,* "Sense is the meaning of a word within a language. Reference is what a word refers to in the world outside language" [188]. From this perspective, it's more useful to think of the poem as a field of meanings than as a thing that means something else, a container for or vehicle of meaning.) Semantic difficulty encompasses figurative difficulty, in which we can't unpack the poem's metaphors, or can't determine what is tenor and what is vehicle, especially when, as is frequently the case, one or the other is omitted, or when the presence and process of figuration are only implied. (This might be called the difficulty of elliptical figuration.) Difficulties interpreting tone, determining the stance and attitude the poem takes and wants the reader to take toward its material, would also fall under the heading of semantic difficulty.

Semantic difficulty can in turn be broken down into difficulty of explication and difficulty of interpretation. Some poems present both kinds of difficulty, some only one or the other. In the case of explicative difficulty, the reader cannot decipher the literal sense of the poem: "What is this poem saying?" One encounters this in Hart Crane's "At Melville's Tomb," and he wrote an extensive explication of the poem for Harriet Monroe, founding editor of *Poetry*. In the case of interpretive difficulty, one grasps what is being said on the literal level, but doesn't know what it means, what it is meant to do. John Ashbery's poems, usually syntactically and explicationally clear, often present this interpretive difficulty. As poet Robert Kelly writes of Ashbery and his "serenely lucid syntax," "it is perfectly easy to understand what he isn't saying." In a different way, and because of their very simplicity and bareness, William Carlos Williams's "This Is Just to Say" and "Poem" ("As the cat / climbed over / the top of // the jamcloset") present extreme cases of interpretive difficulty, in which the "what" is so clear as seemingly to preclude a "why." To say that one doesn't know what a poem means, if one understands its literal sense, is to say that one doesn't know why it's saying what it's saying. The reader asks, "Why am I being told or shown this?"

It is semantic difficulty which readers are usually experiencing when they say, "I don't understand this poem."

Then there is formal difficulty, what John Hollander calls the difficulty of problematical form: one cannot ascertain the poem's shape, cannot hold it in one's head as a construct. Or one cannot determine what kind of poem it is, and thus doesn't know how to read it, in much the same sense that one might try and fail to "read" a person. The reader cannot determine or recognize the formal contract (on the analogy of Hollander's concept of the metrical contract) to which the poem asks him or her to agree. This difficulty is most commonly encountered with poems that play with or violate conventions and expectations, that try to break and/or re-create form: remembering always the intimate relation of form and content, which, as Creeley wrote, are extensions of one another. The question the reader asks is, "What kind of poem is this?"

In the case of formal difficulty, one could add the possibility that the reader understands the terms of the poem's formal contract, but refuses or feels unable to accede to them. Many American poetry readers today, raised on free verse, find it difficult to read metrical and/or rhyming poetry. They can't hear its shape, can't feel its rhythms; its sounds don't make sense to their ears. This type of formal difficulty can be called rhythmic difficulty.

Formal difficulty is a particular case of what George Steiner, cited by Shetley, calls modal difficulty, my final kind. When we experience modal difficulty, "we fail to see a justification for poetic form, the root-occasion of the poem's composition eludes or repels our internalized sense of what poetry should or should not be" (Shetley 7). Steiner actually writes, "what poetry should or should not be about," but I broaden his statement to encompass not just topic or occasion but the poem's status and recognizability as a poem. The two poems by Williams mentioned earlier are prime examples of modal difficulty. To some readers, they are not poems at all, in the same way that Jackson Pollock paintings are not "art" to some viewers. This is another way of saying that those readers lack a frame for these poems. (One often suspects that those same readers, if they accept "The Red Wheelbarrow" as a poem, only do so because it has been taught so often as one; they have been trained to look for its supposed hidden meanings.) Clark Coolidge's poems appear as gibberish to many readers: they present both semantic and modal difficulty. In the case of modal difficulty, a reader asks, "What makes this a poem?"

When people call a poem difficult, they are generally experiencing either semantic difficulty ("I don't know what this poem is saying" or "I don't know why this poem is saying what it's saying"), formal difficulty ("I can't see/hear the shape of this poem"), or modal difficulty ("I don't recognize this as a poem").

Another way to divide up the field would be to distinguish between difficulties of explication (which would include lexical, allusive, and syntactic difficulty), difficulties of interpretation (which would comprise the several varieties of semantic difficulty), and difficulties of recognition (which would encompass both formal and modal difficulty). These categories, of course, can and do overlap to a certain extent.

All of the kinds of difficulty I have enumerated and described are violations of readerly expectations. All readers, no matter how catholic in their tastes and in their knowledge, come to poems with some or another set of expectations. Readers may and do vary widely in their expectations of a poem, and they may have different expectations of different poems and different kinds of poems, but it's impossible to approach a poem as if one were a blank slate, as in the philosophy of John Locke. Shetley points out that "readers' training, expectations, and knowledge have everything to do with whether particular forms of language are experienced as difficult. . . . Different groups of readers have different skills and expectations; allusions familiar to one . . . audience may be mysterious to another, and received conventions that structure the sense of what makes an utterance a poem may vary widely" (6, 9). Every reader encounters poetic difficulty of some kind at some point.

3

Difficulty is not equivalent to complexity. Despite their deceptive surface simplicity, Ben Jonson's poems on the deaths of his children, "On My First Daughter" and "On My First Son," are complex; but they are not difficult. Many of e. e. cummings's more typographically wayward poems are difficult, but not complex. This is another way of saying that they are obscure.

There is a difference between difficulty and obscurity. All obscure poetry is difficult, but (contrary to popular opinion) not all difficult poetry is obscure. Obscurity is a lack of clarity; it is a flaw.*

Difficulty is not a virtue in and of itself, but obscurity is always a defect. Marianne Moore wrote that "one should be as clear as one's own natural reticence allows one to be" ("Idiosyncrasy and Technique" 171). This can be rephrased as, one should be no more difficult than necessary. But it may prove necessary to be very difficult indeed, although there are some poets for whom difficulty is an end in itself, either for the sake of a sense of superiority over the reader or other poets, or for the sake of a sense of rebellion or transgression. Some forms of "difficulty" are as rote as the most well-rehearsed stump speech. I never set out to be "difficult" in my poems, nor do I try to hide things from the reader. Moore asks, "How obscure may one be?" and replies, "I suppose one should not be consciously obscure at all" ("Humility, Concentration, and Gusto," *Marianne Moore Reader* 125).

I take Moore's admonition to refer to the clarity of the materials, of the saying and showing itself, not of what it means or how it's to be interpreted. This is the clarity of an experience: the poem is an experience the reader has, and though one doesn't always know what the experience "means," one knows what happened, what one experienced. But if what happened isn't clear, then there's no possibility of making meaning out of it. Confusion results when the poem's constituent elements are unclear. As poet and critic Joan Houlihan points out, incoherence is neither mysterious nor difficult: it's just another source of boredom. Moore again: "Nor can we dignify confusion by calling it baroque" ("Humility, Concentration, and Gusto," 123). The poet

*Vernon Shetley offers a different distinction between obscurity and difficulty, "using the former term to refer to those elements of language that resist easy semantic processing, and the latter for the reader's response to those elements. Obscurity, then, refers to features within a text, such as allusion, syntactical dislocations, and figurative substitutions, while difficulty refers to something that occurs between reader and text, one kind of possible response to textual obscurity" (5–6). Shetley does not make clear why his terms could not just as easily be reversed (a reader could find a text obscure, hard to see, hard to read, because it is difficult).

should provide the reader with the elements out of which the meaning or meanings can be assembled or produced, and the pieces of the mosaic should be clear and distinct (like Descartes's ideas), even if their relations to one another are not immediately apparent. "Sometimes it appears to candid reflexion that great works of art give no meaning, but give, instead, like the world of nature and history itself, materials whose arrangement suggests a tropism toward meaning, order and form" (Nemerov, "Difficulty of Difficult Poetry" 30).

4

"To read a poem should be an experience, like experiencing an act" (Stevens, "Adagia," *Collected Poetry and Prose* 905). The idea of the artwork as an experience also produces a basis for aesthetic judgment. One can (and should) ask, Does this artwork provide a unique, distinctive experience, one that hasn't already been experienced, known, understood? Walter Benjamin describes shock and distraction as the modern mode of consciousness (or unconsciousness), in which most of our experience is not really experienced, doesn't actually exist for us at all. Although art should be the antidote to this non-experience of distraction, most of what we read simply repeats and re-presents what has already been experienced (or non-experienced). A real work of art makes us stop and pay attention. It breaks through our crust of habit and routine.

I believe that all artists want to communicate with some audience or another, though that potential audience may vary enormously in size and/or kind. If one truly cared nothing about making contact with others, however few or select (not every poem is for every reader, or even for the same reader at every time and in every mood), there would be no reason to make art. One could simply commune with oneself within the confines of one's own mind. But the will to communicate does not define the what or the how of communicating. A poem can communicate itself, in the way that a classical Greek statue or a painting by Willem de Kooning does. This is another way of saying that poems are, or should be, experiences in themselves, and not just accounts of or commentaries on experience; they should be additions to the world, not simply annotations to it. If people think of poems as merely road markers or sign posts to something else, it's no wonder that they don't want to read them. I'd rather go to a place myself than look at a sign pointing out the direction to the place.

Those who define or evaluate a poem in terms of its content are making a serious category mistake. Poems are utterances, but they are first and foremost aesthetic artifacts, events and occasions in language. They often contain propositional statements, but those propositions are, in Susanne Langer's term, sheerly virtual, the form of content, the shape of saying. It is this which distinguishes poetry from most other modes of discourse, in which the expressive or communicative function of language is dominant and in which the materiality of language is suppressed or ignored, or at best used only instrumentally to produce a desired effect in the reader or listener.

As Howard Nemerov has written, "The flat statement that poetry is or ought to be communication, even if it happened to be true, would be uninteresting. Some poetry, not necessarily the most interesting sort, has the clear intention of communicating—meanings. Other poetry has the clear intention of deepening the silence and space about itself. . . . Meanings, generally speaking, are derived from the world and meanings are communicable, but is the world communicable? The work of art imitates in the first place world, it does not immediately imitate meanings except as these occur in the world" ("Difficulty of Difficult Poetry" 29–30).

Walter Pater famously asserted that all art aspires to the condition of music, and the musical analogy is very suggestive. On the one hand, music is intensely expressive, and on the other hand it's hard (at least with instrumental music) to pin down exactly what is being expressed. Also, music is by definition organized and ordered, or it isn't music, just noise or random sound, and the "meaning" of a piece of music is inextricable from its structure. Similarly, a poem means as much through its form, its shape in space and time, as through its content or "subject matter." Poetry is a way of happening, as Auden wrote. The what of saying, though hardly insignificant or irrelevant, is something that poetry shares with any other mode of discourse or expression: it's how a poem happens that sets it apart.

A destination is also an end, but as Nietzsche wrote, the end of a melody isn't its goal. Too often understanding is the prize you get after you've consumed the poem. Now that you've taken it apart to get the decoder ring, you're done with the poem, you can throw it away. I don't see poems as things I want to get over with, any more than I see life as something I want to get over with. The end of life is death, and we start dying from the minute we're born. But on the road to the contagious hospital there are muddy fields full of new growth if we just take the time to look closely. We'll get down that road soon enough. Death is contagious, people are always catching it; the time we don't take will be taken from us. There's no need to hurry oneself along.

I will allow Howard Nemerov the last word. "If poetry reaches the point which chess has reached, where the decisive, profound, and elegant combinations lie within the scope only of masters, and are appreciable only to competent and trained players, that will seem to many people a sorry state of affairs, and to some people a consequence simply of the sinfulness of poets; but it will not in the least mean that poetry is, as they say, dead; rather the reverse. It is when poetry becomes altogether too easy, too accessible, runs down to a few derivative formulae and caters to low tastes and lazy minds—it is then that the life of the art is in danger" ("Difficulty of Difficult Poetry" 30).

WORKS CITED

Collins, Billy. "Poetry, Pleasure, and the Hedonist Reader." *The Eye of the Poet: Six Views of the Art and Craft of Poetry.* Ed. David Citino. New York: Oxford University Press, 2001.

Crystal, David. *How Language Works.* New York: Overlook Press, 2005.

Moore, Marianne. *A Marianne Moore Reader.* New York: Viking, 1961.

Nemerov, Howard. *Reflexions on Poetry and Poetics.* New Brunswick: Rutgers University Press, 1972.

Shetley, Vernon. *After the Death of Poetry: Poet and Audience in Contemporary America.* Durham: Duke University Press, 1993.

Stevens, Wallace. *Collected Poetry and Prose.* Ed. Frank Kermode and Joan Richardson. New York: The Library of America, 1997.

Scattered Thoughts on Fracture

Despite its many accomplishments over the past century or more, I grow weary of poetic experimentation for its own sake. By now it has frequently come to seem like a form of keeping up with fashion: never wear the same outfit twice, make sure you're wearing next season's clothes. This is part of what Jack Spicer means when he writes to the long-dead Federico García Lorca that "invention is merely the enemy of poetry." Those trendy outfits also strikingly resemble the clothes they wore in the 1910s and '20s (many things new are old), which too many people too often forget. As Mexican poet Octavio Paz noted in the mid-1960s, "the avant-garde of 1967 repeats the deeds and gestures of those of 1917." So many of the "experiments" in which our avant-garde engage were performed by Eliot, Pound, Moore, Williams, et alia, long before any of our current practitioners were born. There's nothing wrong with using techniques that have already been developed (the English language is one of those techniques, after all), but there's something unseemly about claiming that you invented them yesterday.

Forms have no intrinsic values, but they have contextual meanings: as James Longenbach notes, "The relationship between formal choice and ideological position is constantly shifting, and it isn't possible to predict the repercussions of formal decisions except inasmuch as we might see them played out in the work of individual poets" (95). Allen Grossman notes that forms are stained or given meaning by certain performances of them. The Modernists, let alone the poets who preceded them (both those who inspired them and those with whom they struggled), cannot be merely wished away. "You cannot experiment with only the history of experimentation as your archive," in Ann Lauterbach's acute admonition (65).

The avant-garde frequently forgets that Pound's injunction to "make it new" contains two parts. They concentrate so much on trying to be new (which ends up as a cult of novelty that mirrors the planned obsolescence of the consumer culture it claims to critique, a consumer culture my main criticism of which is that it isn't in fact available to all) that they neglect the necessity to make something, that newness is not a value in itself (no human being is "new," though each person is unique) but a means to the rejuvenation of aesthetic experience (and thus, analogously, of our experience of and in the world). Ann Lauterbach points out that "in re/citations of Ezra Pound's injunction to 'make it new,' emphasis has invariably fallen on the word 'new,' the word which most conjures the operations of commerce. We have been in thrall to the new, even as it has worn itself through with recyclings, a kind of *déja new,* which has exhausted our attention and made us all victims of fashion. As Jean-François Lyotard says, 'Hidden in the cynicism of innovation is certainly the despair that nothing further will happen.' We have ignored the other two words, 'make' and 'it,' as if they were of no significance" (44).

Though it has produced some wonderful works of art, fracture has become too easy, even evasive: it's become simply another style. Rather than just cutting things up or claiming that they just are cut up (a reductive view of art as a reflection of the world shared by many avant-garde writers, at least in America), it's much more difficult and interesting to put things together despite or in the face of fragmentation, not to create false wholes or a false confidence in wholes, but to see and show that things are related, however random their surfaces may appear. That randomness is an ideological illusion, and this is as much the Marx in me as the John Crowe Ransom. Marx wrote in the *Grundrisse* of the distinction between the apparently real and the actually real, the chaotic, disconnected surfaces of the world and the interrelated, interconnected whole (however riven and fissured) which that world actually comprises. In Terry Eagleton's explication, "It is a mistake to equate concreteness with things. An individual object is the unique phenomenon it is because it is caught up in a mesh of relations with other objects. It is this web of relations and interactions . . .

which is 'concrete,' while the object considered in isolation is purely abstract" (142).

Totalities are always contradictory, but they are totalities, and we live in, among, and with them. Part of the work of thought and the work of poetry is to trace out their lineaments: poetry, language, and thought are about producing and revealing relation, about making connections among disparate things often seen as disconnected or even opposed or contradictory: contradiction and opposition are also modes of relation. Barbara K. Fischer notes in *The Boston Review* of some of the transgressive or subversive claims of "experimental" writing that "from the vantage point of our current historical-political moment, 'sense, order, and coherence' don't seem like such terrible things," and goes on to warn against "the dangers of enshrining yet another chaos that cannot redeem itself."

Emerson wrote that "I am a fragment," but a fragment is always a fragment of something. Our experience is (falsely) fractured, atomized, and my self (like my society) is likewise fractured and atomized, in pieces. ("My mind is in pieces, but at least I know what the pieces are," as my friend Ed Mathews once wrote me: lucky man.) But it is also a whole, of a piece, a complex unity of contradictions. As Fredric Jameson writes in "Reflections in Conclusion," the afterword to the Frankfurt School compilation *Aesthetics and Politics,* "An aesthetic of novelty today . . . must seek desperately to renew itself by ever more rapid rotations of its own axis. . . . When modernism and its accompanying techniques of 'estrangement' have become the dominant style whereby the consumer is reconciled with capitalism, the habit of fragmentation itself needs to be 'estranged' and corrected by a more totalizing way of viewing phenomena" (211). Paul Hoover puts it another way in his essay "Murder and Closure: On the Impression of Reality in American Poetry" (included in his collection *Fables of Representation*) when he asks, "If this interruptiveness is inspired by electronic mass media, which is controlled by powerful capitalist interests, how is such a literature revolutionary?" (14). Far from being transgressive or subversive, it becomes just another social symptom and reflection.

I don't want my work merely to mirror my state, or my State (that would only be another representational aesthetic), but to do something with those things. It's much more difficult to articulate things together than just to toss out the pieces and say, "Nothing can be done with this," or even, "I have seen the future and it is broken." I am interested, as a person and as a writer, in how things relate to one another. As Jack Spicer wrote to Robin Blaser, "Things fit together. . . . Two inconsequential things can combine together to become a consequence." My interest in syntax, the relation of words and phrases to one another, arises from the desire to make or reveal connections among the elements of my poems and my world(s). My questions are always, "How can these things be put together? What constellation do they form?" Which is not to claim that a reconciliation of self and society, or self and self, can be effected in or by means of language.

WORKS CITED

Eagleton, Terry. *How to Read a Poem.* New York: Wiley-Blackwell, 2006.

Hoover, Paul. *Fables of Representation: Essays.* Ann Arbor: University of Michigan Press, 2004.

Jameson, Fredric. "Reflections in Conclusion." *Aesthetics and Politics.* Trans. and ed. Ronald Taylor. London: Verso, 1980.

Lauterbach, Ann. *The Night Sky: Writings on the Poetics of Experience.* New York: Viking, 2005.

Longenbach, James. *The Art of the Poetic Line.* St. Paul: Graywolf Press, 2007.

Defining "Post-Avant-Garde" Poetry

The phrase "post-avant poetry," which was coined either seriously by Ron Silliman or parodically by Joan Houlihan, is bandied about quite a bit in the online poetry world. (I've never seen the phrase in print, an indication of how separate the two realms often are, though many people participate in both.) It's used with the assumption that "we all know what that is," but the term is rarely defined. Here follows my attempt to pin down a term much-mentioned but seldom specified, with the caveat that Stephen Burt makes in a postscript to his essay on what he calls "The Elliptical Poets": "People who follow the arts like to talk about schools; often they prefer talking about schools and trends to talking about individual poets and their poems" (48). I hope that this too-broad discussion is not taken as a substitute for discussing actual poets and actual poems.

"Post-avant" (as in "post-avant-garde"—insider groups love shorthand) poets can be described as writers who, at their best, have imbibed the lessons of the Modernists and their successors in what might be called the experimental or avant-garde stream of American poets, including the Objectivists (especially Oppen and Zukofsky), what have been called the New American Poetries, particularly the Projectivist/Black Mountain School and the New York School(s), from Jack Spicer and Robert Duncan to John Ashbery and Frank O'Hara, and the Language poets (including such poets and polemicists as Charles Bernstein and Ron Silliman), without feeling the need (as so many other poetic formations have) to pledge allegiance to a particular group identity (the poetry world is full of fence-building and turf wars) or a particular mode of proceeding artistically. As poet Elizabeth Willis writes in her artist's statement in my anthology *Lyric Postmodernisms,* "Part of what's so interesting about the current moment is its refusal of an overtly oedipal relation to literary traditions on either the right or the left, and a willingness to construct and invent not only new kinds of poetry but new ways of reading" (259).

These poets don't form a movement, let alone a school, but something more like a set of tendencies. As Stephen Burt writes, "Whether a school exists, or where its boundaries lie, seem . . . questions both less profound, and less durable, than the questions we ask about each poet and about individual poems. At the same time individual poems may respond to their historical moment and invoke their stylistic [formal, and thematic] affinities with other poems" (50).

Poet and editor Rebecca Wolff writes of the work in her online journal *Fence*, a home of the post-avant (along with such journals as *Boston Review, Colorado Review, Denver Quarterly, New American Writing, Verse,* and *Volt* and such publishers as Ahsahta Press, the University of California Press, the late lamented University of Georgia Press Contemporary Poetry Series, and Wesleyan University Press), that such writing "intentionally blurs the distinction between 'difficulty' and 'accessibility,' preferring instead to address a continuum of utterance." Though many of these poets have projects and even systems (the book, as distinct from or even opposed to the individual poem, is important in much of their work), there aren't a lot of programs. There's much prose writing and thinking about poetry, and there are many, many blogs (this is a very wired "generation," and much sense of post-avant poetic community is produced online), but not many manifestoes. (Flarf, which poet Kasey Mohammad has defined as "intentionally bad poetry that involves Google search text results," a deliberate anti-poetry based on what Dan Hoy has called "poetics of awfulness as a style," is probably not "post-avant," but I don't understand it well enough to discuss it.) And no doubt I've missed a lot—there's a lot to miss.

In his 1997 article "The New Modernism" (reprinted in his essay collection *Fables of Representation*), poet and editor Paul Hoover writes that "compositional complexity and a renewed emphasis on abstraction are the cornerstones of the new modernism. It has some of the difficulty of modernism but little of its commitment to history and myth. [RS: I would disagree with this. I would say that it has a different relationship to history and myth, not relying upon them as sources of authority but as fields of what Foucault called the archaeology of knowledge.] In its love of the fragment, mosaic organization, broken sequences, and appropriation, the new modernism also resembles the old. What differs is the gender and ethnicity of the poets involved" (138). That is to say, the new modernism is much more diverse in terms of gender, race, and ethnicity (though not necessarily of class) than the old Modernism ever was or wanted to be. Hoover's category of "the new modernism" is much more broad than my notion of the "post-avant-garde," as he traces out two branches. The first branch includes "poets like Ann Lauterbach, Marjorie Welish, Michael Palmer, Jorie Graham, Rosmarie Waldrop, Nathaniel Mackey, Donald Revell, and Bob Perelman [RS: this seems an odd assemblage to me, at least in terms of professed and apparent poetic lineages] whose work contains figured abstraction and, at times, sustained lyrical argument and are influenced by the romantic lineage of postmodernism including Ashbery and Duncan." The second branch includes "poets like Lyn Hejinian, Susan Howe, Bruce Andrews, Ron Silliman, and Charles Bernstein whose origins are in Gertrude Stein, objectivism, and Charles Olson and employ a more discontinuous compositional program" (139). I would call this a distinction between romantic and anti-romantic Modernist lineages, between a lyric postmodernist mode and an anti-lyrical postmodernist mode. I would place most of the poets I consider as "post-avant garde" within the former lineage and mode, however much they query and sometimes explode (from the inside) romanticism and lyricism.

Poet and critic Stephen Burt's invention of a school of so-called Elliptical poetry, including such diverse poets as Lucie Brock-Broido, Forrest Gander, August Kleinzahler, Thylias Moss, Karen Volkman, and C. D. Wright, has been much talked-about, including in a symposium in the journal *American Letters and Commentary*. Burt writes in his 1999 essay "The Elliptical Poets" that "Elliptical Poets are always hinting, punning, or swerving away from a never-quite-unfolded backstory; they are easier to process in parts than in wholes. They believe provisionally in identities (in one or *more* 'I' per poem), but they suspect the I's they invoke: they admire disjunction and confrontation, but they know how [a] little can go a long way. Elliptics seek the authority of the rebellious; they want to challenge their readers, violate decorum, surprise or explode assumptions about what belongs in a poem, or what matters in life, and to do so while meeting traditional lyric goals. Their favorite attitudes are desperately extravagant, or tough-guy terse, or defiantly childish: they don't believe in, or seek, a judicious tone" (41). Burt goes on to write that "all [Elliptical poets] want to convey *both* metaphysical challenge *and* recognizable, seen or tasted, detail. Ellipticism rejects: poems written in order to demonstrate theories; prettiness as its own end; slogans; mysticism; straight-up narrative; and extended abstraction. [RS: Contrarily, I would say that one distinguishing feature of post-avant-garde poetry is its interest and even its investment in exploring abstraction as a mode and a theme, something that Paul Hoover touches on in the passage quoted above.] Ellipticals are uneasy about (less often, hostile to) inherited elites and privileges, but they are not populists, and won't write down to, or connect the dots for, their readers; their difficulty conveys respect." (This last assertion is echoed and complicated by Rebecca Wolff's comment noted above.)

Burt's Ellipticist poets seem to have in common only a set of surface effects: they all write flashy poems. Indeed, many of them have queried if not rejected their assigned membership in this school. Cole Swensen, for example, asserts in "Elliptical Poetry: A Response," that Burt "is listing traits that have been present in various innovative writing communities for decades and attributing them to a very narrow, and relatively both conservative and recent, group of writers" (66). And I am not sure what makes these specifically "elliptical." My *Merriam-Webster's Dictionary* defines "elliptical" as "a : of, relating to, or marked by ellipsis or an ellipsis [in turn defined as 'a: the omission of one or more words that are obviously understood but that must be supplied to make a construction grammatically complete, or b: a sudden leap from one topic to another']; b (1): of, relating to, or marked by extreme economy of speech or writing (2): of or relating to deliberate obscurity (as of literary or conversational style)." As Burt describes his "Ellipticist" poets, none of these definitions seems particularly to apply, at least no more than they would to any number of poets from John Donne to Emily Dickinson to John Berryman to Ann Lauterbach (whom he does not mention).

In "Shearing Away," an earlier version of his essay that appeared in the Spring 1998 issue of the British journal *Poetry Review,* Burt admits to having made up this *soi-disant* "school." Later, in clarifying what he means by "school," he writes that "Ellipticism counts as a school of a movement in the way that 'metaphysical poetry' or 'confessional poetry' count as movements, not in the way that 'language writing' or the Black Arts Movement or New Formalism (each of which had manifestos) count as movements; the so-called [by Burt himself] Ellipticals (like the so-called metaphysicals) need not have signed a manifesto, or appeared in one place at one time, in order to share the aesthetic goals I have described" (49). I would say that they share at most aesthetic tendencies and styles, rather than goals, which are always difficult to decipher in any case.

As Cole Swensen points out, "Historically, a school is based on more than observable surface similarities. . . . Sometimes, in fact, the members of a given group have differed widely in their works' appearances, approaches, and other immediate aspects, and have based their affinity instead on much broader aesthetic issues, as well as, at times, shared social and political convictions and some degree of shared experience. As the term has been used throughout the century, a school is a spontaneous and accidental situation that laces people together as it laces art into individual lives. . . . Using the term at this point in history does imply those extra-textual affinities, which I'm not sure are appropriate here" (65). Swensen also points out the ways in which Burt's map seems "if not to construct, then at least to arrange [the] territory before it sets out to guide us through it" (65): it draws factional lines in advance through a future that hasn't yet arrived.

In a recent *New York Times* review of Matthea Harvey's new book *Modern Life,* critic David Orr concurs with Burt's description, but he frames it in pejorative terms. Orr writes that Harvey works in "a variation on the trendiest contemporary style, which relies heavily on disconnected phrases, abrupt syntactical shifts, attention-begging titles ('The Gem Is on Page Sixty-Four'), quirky diction ('orangery,' 'aigrettes'), flickering italics, oddball openings ('The scent of pig is faint tonight') and a tone ranging from daffy to plangent—basically, two scoops of John Ashbery and a sprinkling of Gertrude Stein. It's not hard to write acceptable poetry in this mode." While this description is true of many writers (any mode has its better and its worse practitioners, and mediocrity is the norm in any field of endeavor), I don't find it fair as an overall evaluation. In fact, Orr's review of Harvey's work is quite positive. As he points out, "If it's relatively easy to write passable poetry in the style du jour, it's never easy to write good poetry in any style," which seems to me much more to the point.

Some of these writers have been called "third way" writers by Ron Silliman, who has written that "younger poets today I think have more of an opportunity of learning from all worlds without having to sign up & pick sides. And that in turn will itself impact how writing gets done, going forward." However, Silliman distinguishes what he calls "third way" writing (among whose practitioners he numbers Forrest Gander, Jorie Graham, Robert Hass [whose avant-garde inclinations I don't see], and Ann Lauterbach, as well as the much younger Graham Foust), which exemplifies "a post-militant American poetics," from "post-avant" writing, saying that "third way" poetry is dependent on the dichotomy between what he calls post-avant poetry and what he pejoratively calls "School of Quietude" poetry: "The Third Way has always struck me as predicated upon the existence of the other two." This indicates that he still maintains a distinction between vanguardist and rear-guardist contemporary American poetry, one that I believe no longer applies.

Critic and poet Calvin Bedient, whom Joshua Corey has called "one of the most passionate advocates of a return to lyric modernism in contemporary poetry," has briefly referred to this kind of poetry as "soft" avant-garde, as distinct from the hard (and didactic) kind still associated with (what remains of) Language writing. I have called some of their work, after Wittgenstein, "lyrical investigations" in the introduction to my anthology *Lyric Postmodernisms.*

Post-avant writers tend to eschew the standard and standardized autobiographical or pseudo-autobiographical anecdote which predominates in what's called (usually pejoratively) "mainstream" poetry. Indeed, they frequently problematize and question the notions of self and of personal experience. But they don't just discard the self as some kind of ideological illusion. As well, they tend to avoid or at least seriously complicate narrative, often breaking story down into its component parts. They incorporate fracture and disjunction without enthroning it as a ruling principle (poet Cynthia Cruz calls much of this work "the broken lyric"). They swerve away from traditional notions of coherence and unity, perhaps fearing that too closed or complete a totality is false or overbearing. In a way, their work is a version of the "leaping poetry" proposed by Robert Bly in the 1960s, a poetry which proceeds by associational rather than linear logic and does not stop, or stoop, to explain. They are interested in exploring, interrogating, and sometimes exploding language, identity, and society, without giving up on the pleasures, challenges, and resources of the traditional lyric. Their work combines the lyric's creative impulse with the critical, deconstructive project of Language poetry, engaging the dialectic of what critic Charles Altieri calls lyricism and lucidity and what, earlier, W. H. Auden called enchantment and disenchantment, without settling on one side or the other.

As Stephen Burt has said, they are "trying to figure out how to incorporate both lyric and non- (if not anti-) lyric impulses, and trying . . . to put modernist fragmentation together with Romantic expectations about voice and form," and without any preconceptions about what forms such a potential synthesis might take. Theirs is a magpie-like eclecticism, that draws from whatever materials, traditions, and techniques are of interest and of use, however seemingly incompatible, however ideologically opposed historically. They don't try to destroy the past for the sake of the future, or trumpet teleological notions of artistic "progress" or "advance," though they are fascinated with the processes of poetic construction. As poet Robert Archambeau has recently written, "The post-avant seems to have very little interest in making grand claims of any kind: not only does it eschew a sense of heroic poetic progress, but it eschews big political or spiritual claims." Perhaps this is a reflection of the postmodern rejection or at least suspicion of grand narratives and transcendental signifiers.

This cross-fertilization has been happening in American poetry for a long time, but there are many people on various "sides" who either don't see it or vehemently oppose it, perhaps because it undermines their own carefully constructed identity formations (which many of them conceive of as having been forged under fire). Hard-core avant-gardistes, as well as hard-core defenders of a narrow and reified "tradition," are at this point both ideologically and aesthetically backward: they're still fighting the poetry cold wars. But as editor Christopher Beach writes in the introduction to *Artifice and Indeterminacy,* his "anthology of new poetics," "Any such unqualified agenda of poetic and institutional identification [as Donald M. Allen proclaimed when he pronounced that all the poets included in *The New American Poetry* shared 'a total rejection of all those qualities typical of academic verse'] would seem inappropriate and somewhat naïve; we have seen the blurring of such clear distinctions as those between 'academic' and 'non-academic' schools of poetry, between institutional structures and avant-garde communities, between insiders and outsiders" (vii).

The avant-garde isn't the advance guard anymore, and hasn't been for a while. The armies have been disbanded, though many of the officers have yet to inform themselves of the fact. There are, of course, many people who haven't yet passed through the avant-garde and never will. (It would be nice if some of those people would at least read Eliot. But then, it would be nice if some of those people would read Keats.) But once you have passed through that avant-garde door, there is no forward march, no destination or telos, just an open field. In the somewhat exaggerated words of philosopher and art critic Arthur C. Danto, "There are to be no next things. The time for next things is past. [RS: nice paradox.] It [is] like coming to the end of the world with no more continents to discover. One must now begin to make habitable the only continents that there are" (217). Visual artist–turned-poet Kenneth Goldsmith, who might or might not accept a characterization as a "post-avant" poet, writes on the Poetry Foundation's "Harriet Blog" that "Language Poetry put the period on the end of the modernist sentence. If you're playing an innovative game, after Language Poetry, there's no more deconstructive work to do. That project has finished. The next step then becomes a reconstructive project that sees language as a whole again—moving information—but, like certain strains of postmodernism, acknowledges the cracks in the newly reformed linguistic vessel."

Only because of the backwardness of literature in comparison to music and visual art can self-appointed avant-gardistes still feel themselves in the forefront of artistic morality. In other areas of artistic endeavor, the idea of vanguard art, art in step with the progress of history, and the conviction that some artistic practices are more correct, even more virtuous, has been rather thoroughly abandoned. Goldsmith wryly notes that "I often use [William S. Burroughs collaborator] Brion Gysin's quote from 1959 that poetry is 50 years behind painting." As philosopher and literary theorist Daniel Barbiero writes of "the willingness of contemporary poets to use a spectrum of devices without undue prejudice" (87) in *Telling It Slant,* an anthology of "avant-garde poetics of the 1990s": "To anyone who has followed the visual arts during the past two decades or so, or academic music in the decade prior to that, the notion of an avant-garde [RS: however or even whether one would define such a thing at this historical juncture] without agonism will not seem very strange" (87). Arthur C. Danto (as I have indicated above), in such books as *After the End of Art, Beyond the Brillo Box,* and *The State of the Art,* and music critic Alex Ross, in his brilliant book *The Rest Is Noise: Listening to the Twentieth Century,* both make this point about, respectively, visual art and music. Ross's book includes a wonderful 1992 quote from composer John Cage, whose avant-garde credentials are impeccable: "We live in a time I think not of mainstream, but of many streams, or even, if you insist upon a river of time, that we have come to a delta, maybe even beyond delta to an ocean which is going back to the skies" (341). This image of a spatial expanse rather than a road or path leading to a definite future destination, even if one not known in advance, echoes Danto's geographical metaphor in my preceding paragraph.

Obviously, experimentation and innovation will and should

continue, in the sense of trying something out to see what happens, of engaging in poetic endeavors without knowing or attempting to predetermine the outcome. Poetry is always at least in part a foray into the unknown, a project of finding out what happens in the process of participating in its happening. But the sense of a forward march, of a correct path to the future and a virtuous method by which to reach to that future, is gone, or at least no longer valid. To what destination are the arts, is poetry, marching at this very late date?

As Joshua Clover writes in "Poem," "We lie down in categories / And wake up in concepts" (6). It's important to remember that the poets I describe are very diverse and individually distinctive. That's what makes their work interesting and worth discussing. But their work broadly and variously shares common characteristics that make it a significant area of contemporary poetic activity. There are doubtless many "post-avant" poets who would not recognize themselves in this description. Some would even vehemently reject my description (practitioners of flarf might do so), and some wouldn't consider themselves "post-avant" at all. Paul Hoover points out that slam, spoken word, and performance poetry constitute an almost entirely separate world from that of print poetry, aesthetically, conceptually, and materially, with its own networks and institutions. Given that particularity, I don't attempt to discuss it here.

Some established poets whose work maps out or creates this third space are Michael Anania, Paul Auster (though I don't know if he still writes poetry), Bruce Beasley, Martine Bellen, Mei-mei Berssenbrugge, Lucie Brock-Broido, Killarney Clary, Gillian Conoley, Carolyn Forché, Kathleen Fraser, Alice Fulton, Forrest Gander, C. S. Giscombe, Peter Gizzi, Jorie Graham, Brenda Hillman, Claudia Keelan, Ann Lauterbach, Timothy Liu, Jane Miller, Michael Palmer, Suzanne Paola, John Peck, Dennis Phillips, Bin Ramke, Stephen Ratcliffe, Donald Revell, Martha Ronk, Peter Sacks, Aaron Shurin, Carol Snow, Susan Stewart, Cole Swensen, Rosmarie Waldrop, Marjorie Welish, Elizabeth Willis, and C. D. Wright. Most of these writers are included in my book *Lyric Postmodernisms: An Anthology of Contemporary Innovative Poetries.*

Some "emerging" or less-established poets who work in this space are Christopher Arigo, Dan Beachy-Quick, Jasper Bernes, Laynie Browne, Brigitte Byrd, Julie Carr, Jeff Clark, Joshua Clover, Joshua Corey, Cynthia Cruz, Jocelyn Emerson, Amy England, Lisa Fishman, Graham Foust, John Gallaher, Michele Glazer, Noah Eli Gordon, Matthea Harvey, Brian Henry, Joan Houlihan, Christine Hume, Catherine Imbriglio, Julie Kalendek, Joanna Klink, Joshua Kryah, Joseph Lease, Malinda Markham, Mark McMorris, Rusty Morrison, Jenny Mueller, Laura Mullen, Amy Newman, Geoffrey Nutter, Geoffrey G. O'Brien, Tracy Philpot, D. A. Powell, Heather Ramsdell, Rebecca Reynolds, Brenda Shaughnessy, 'Annah Sobelman, Brian Teare, Karen Volkman, G. C. Waldrep, Joshua Marie Wilkinson, Tyrone Williams, Sam Witt, Andrew Zawacki, and Rachel Zucker. Many of these writers are included in my *Iowa Anthology of New American Poetries,* published by the University of Iowa Press in 2004.

This is not meant to be a comprehensive list, or even a list of all the poets whose work I enjoy who write "that kind of poetry" (as Joan Houlihan writes that editors refer to it), but just the starting point for a discussion of a phenomenon much mentioned but rarely defined or described, one that poet and critic Joshua Corey proposes as "the new American mainstream, retaining whatever oppositional force it still possesses only through institutional memory—though it still stands strongly enough as a bulwark against the laziness and anti-intellectualism of the genuine mainstream of American cultural life."

There are many people who believe (or act as if they believe) that we still live in the stultified and stultifying poetic culture of the 1950s (in which there was still more going on than people choose to remember or credit), and cultivate a sense of themselves as rebels against a monolithic literary orthodoxy that no longer exists, if it ever really did. As intellectual historian Peter Gay points out in his book *Modernism: The Lure of Heresy,* if the bourgeois audience had really been as monolithically or rigidly philistine as they were and have since been portrayed as being, then Modernism would never have become successful, let alone institutionalized.

Many maintain this sense of themselves as marginalized outsiders, if not downright victims, no matter how comfortably ensconced they are within what Louis Althusser (a highly problematic thinker who nonetheless produced some useful ideas) called the ideological state apparatus of higher education, or just within the literary world in general. (It also needs reminding that, closely entwined as they are in the current American situation, academia and the literary world are not identical.) As the wonderful poet Michael Anania once said to me, if you continue to cultivate a sense of grievance and victimization once you become successful (or if you were never an outsider to begin with, as is the case with many people who identify themselves as transgressors and subversives), then you just become a jerk. (He used a stronger word, but I'm trying to be polite.)

I close with a quote from poet Brenda Hillman's essay "On Song, Lyric, and Strings," about the nature, place, and role of the lyric in today's "post"-everything world, from which I also quote in my introduction to *Lyric Postmodernisms:*

> Current aesthetic quarrels and conversations between poets are real enough, and the aesthetically abstract or non-referential lyric poetry may have a different readership from poetry that announces its purposes in more narrative styles, but these issues should concern poets far less than keeping poetry alive in a culture of appalling greed, a culture that doesn't read much of anything, a culture that does business as usual in a time of Enron and retributionist wars.

Would that more people could keep these wise words in mind.

WORKS CITED

Barbiero, Daniel. "Avant-Garde without Agonism?" *Telling It Slant: Avant-Garde Poetics of the 1990s.* Ed. Mark Wallace and Steven Marks. Tuscaloosa: University of Alabama Press, 2002.

Beach, Christopher, ed. *Artifice and Indeterminacy: An Anthology of New Poetics.* Tuscaloosa: University of Alabama Press, 1998.

Burt, Stephen. "The Elliptical Poets." Reprinted in *A Poetry Criticism Reader.* Ed. Jerry Harp and Jan Weismiller. Iowa City: University of Iowa Press, 2006.

Clover, Joshua. *The Totality for Kids.* Berkeley: University of California Press, 2006.

Danto, Arthur C. *The State of the Art.* New York: Prentice Hall, 1987.

Gay, Peter. *Modernism: The Lure of Heresy.* New York: W. W. Norton, 2008

Hoover, Paul. *Fables of Representation: Essays.* Ann Arbor: University of Michigan Press, 2004.

Orr, David. Review of Matthea Harvey, *Modern Life.* http://www.nytimes.com/2008/02/17/books/review/Orr2-t.html?_r=2&oref=slogin&oref=slogin.

Ross, Alex. *The Rest Is Noise: Listening to the Twentieth Century.* New York: Farrar, Straus and Giroux, 2007.

Shepherd, Reginald, ed. *The Iowa Anthology of New American Poetries.* Iowa City: University of Iowa Press, 2004.

Shepherd, Reginald, ed. *Lyric Postmodernisms: An Anthology of Contemporary Innovative Poetries.* Denver: Counterpath Press, 2008.

Swensen, Cole. "Elliptical Poetry: A Response." *American Letters and Commentary* 11, 1999.

Wallace, Mark, and Steven Marks, eds. *Telling It Slant: Avant-Garde Poetics of the 1990s.* Tuscaloosa: University of Alabama Press, 2002.

Wolff, Rebecca, ed. *Fence.* http://www.fenceportal.org.

“Only in the Light of Lost Words Can We Imagine Our Rewards”

On John Ashbery’s Some Trees

Some Trees, John Ashbery’s first regularly published collection, contains numerous poems that explore how the artistic consciousness relates to the world in which it finds itself and what that consciousness makes of the world it is given. In his examinations of how it feels to think, and of how thought and feeling interact with the world to make art, Ashbery is an heir of Wallace Stevens, whom he has called, along with early Auden and Laura Riding, one of “the writers who most formed my language as a poet.”

As I reread the book’s title poem, it seems to me in many ways a response to Wallace Stevens’s “The Snow Man.” In both poems, an object or group of objects in the material world, arbitrarily chosen and yet significant because of that choice, is the occasion for a meditation on how to live in that world, how to make one’s way through a world not of one’s making. In Stevens’s poem, one “must” have a winter’s mind, the mind of a man made of snow (which is to say, a man who is not a man at all), to look out on the winter landscape and perceive no misery there, in the sound of the wind and the leaves in the wind. But what does “must” mean? That one should have such a mind, that one should turn such a colder eye upon the world, declining to invest it with feeling and meaning? Or that only an actual snow man, “nothing himself,” at one with his wintry landscape (indeed, a feature of that landscape), could so see the world, perceiving “Nothing that is not there and the nothing that is.” Given how much of something the poem presents us (nothing is nothing to see), asks us to behold, I would settle upon the latter point of view.

"Some Trees" presents a friendlier landscape, although an equally contingent one. These are, after all, only "some" trees: there is no guarantee that any other trees will offer such muted epiphanies, or even that these trees would do so on a different morning. "These are amazing." These and no other trees? Or would any group of trees so amaze, if looked at properly? (I am reminded that for William Carlos Williams, poetry was a mode of attention, and anything could become a poem if paid the right sort of attention.) These trees are amazing in part because they are in relation, "each / Joining a neighbor." As Nietzsche wrote, before there can be one, there must be two, for one can only exist by being distinguished from another. That everything connects is a never-ceasing source of wonder. And these mute trees speak, their "still performance" a silent analogue of speech. In his sonnet "Correspondences," another poem about relation, Baudelaire wrote that Nature is a living temple from whose pillars confused words issue forth. Are not these trees, some trees at least, such pillars in Nature's temple?

And we have arranged to meet by accident (a throw of the dice will never abolish chance, as Mallarmé has reminded us) far from the world and yet wholly within it, agreeing with its speaking picture, its silent discourse. As far from the world as agreeing with it is very close indeed, though never fully there (can we ever be fully there, fully present?), on this morning which seems full of possibility, as beginnings always seem to be. And suddenly we are "what the trees try // to tell us we are," though the poem never tells us what that is (to do so might shut down possibility), or even who "we" are. The poem is intimate (every reader is invited to be part of this "we," like these trees each joining its neighbor) and yet distant, from the world, from any reader (who is this we of whom we are not only invited but assumed to be part?). The trees, after all, are together yet apart: rooted in place, they cannot move any closer to one another or, for that matter, any further apart.

But these trees mean something, or so that is what they try to tell us, whoever we are. But how do we know what they are trying to tell us, or that they are trying to tell us anything? It is in this way that the poem responds to "The Snow Man": it is, after all, "a winter morning," and the days are "Placed in a puzzling light" not unlike Stevens's "distant glitter // Of the January sun," cold light in which one sees "the junipers shagged with ice, / The spruces rough" in that distant glitter. More trees seen in winter light, some trees and not other trees (pine trees, junipers, spruces). The trees in Ashbery's winter morning are probably bare too, perhaps also crusted with snow, shagged with ice. And maybe it is morning in Stevens's poem, the sun not rising far above the horizon all day.

We behold some trees and they mean to us, we hear some wind and it means to us. We are not snow men. In Stevens's poem, what we see is the burden the bare trees bear, but also the beauty of that burden: cold pastoral. What we hear in the wind's sound, in the sound of the leaves the wind carries and drops, carries and drops, is misery. One must have a mind of winter not to hear it, and who has such a mind? Not the speaker of this poem. In Ashbery's, we see those trees and somehow hear them too. They mean, but what they mean is the possibility of joy: "soon / We may touch, love, explain." Not now, and not certainly, but we may, and we may soon. (This seems a bright and sunny winter morning, cold but invigorating.) The words that issue from Nature's pillars are after all confused, but that's to be expected when speech has become a still performance, or rather, when it is as though a still performance were speech, as though speech had become such a *tableau vivant.*

We have not invented such loveliness (the loveliness of hope, the beauty of potential), and we are glad not to have. It is something beyond us, an outside that confirms and consoles us. It surrounds us, a comfort but also a constraint: contra Schopenhauer, the world is not all will and idea. As Stevens writes in his "Adagia," "All of our ideas come from the natural world: Trees = umbrellas." Or at least some trees do, a shelter from the rain or even from the snow.

The silence is already filled with noises (the noise of the wind, perhaps, of a few leaves in the wind, some leaves). The world around us, this little piece of it, this place in which we have arranged to find ourselves, to meet one another and our world by chance, is "A canvas on which emerges / A chorus of smiles" (the synesthesia is, I think deliberate, the speech of a still performance, some trees' soundless urgings). It is "a winter morning, / Placed in puzzling light": we can experience but never wholly understand the world; the light discloses but does not explain. And it is moving: we are moved, whoever we are this morning, but the world is moving too, life is all motion. "Minute by minute they change," writes Yeats; and Stevens reminds us that the blackbird whirling in the autumn winds (so close to winter, yet so far) is just a small part of the pantomime. The days are reticent, at least our days are reticent—or rather, our days have put on such reticence (this reticence that tells us so much once we choose to really listen, so much we have not invented but we have definitely interpreted). We may soon touch, love, explain (all these things that trees can't do, not some trees, not any trees), but when we don't know, or even if these things will happen at all. Right here, right now, these implications, innuendos, inflections of morning light seem sufficient: "These accents seem their own defense." What else can be expected of the world but hints? That the world should speak at all, however reticently, in however puzzling a winter morning light, is enough, is amazing indeed.

Poems call to poems. The sestina "A Painter" takes up the imagery, tone, and themes of "The Idea of Order at Key West," presenting us with a male painter (or rather, a painter manqué) as distinct from a female singer, but also with the same question that Stevens addresses in a letter, "whether a poem about a natural object is roused by the natural object or whether the natural object is clothed with its poetic characteristics by the poet." The two poems appear to arrive at different answers to this perpetual question of poetry, of art itself, but they are not so far apart as they at first appear, both lingering by the seashore as they do.

In Stevens's poem, the unnamed woman sang "beyond the genius of the sea." The water was not fully shaped by her imagination or her voice, but the motion of its waves and tides, pattern calling to pattern (like those trees telling us what we might do, what we might do), "Made constant cry . . . , / That was not ours although we understood," and part of what we understood is that this voice is "Inhuman, of the veritable [that is, true] ocean." "The sea was not a mask," not a projection of human desires and fears, a screen of human meaning. "No more was she." She was a woman walking by the ocean, singing what she heard, which was both the sea and her own voice. "But it was she and not the sea we heard." She was, as Stevens writes, "the maker of the song she sang." The sea was her locale. But still we heard "the dark voice of the sea," and more than that, her voice and more than that, our own voices and more than that. The sounds of water and wind were "meaningless plungings" out of which we made and make meaning. Her song she made out of the sounds she heard made us see and hear the world more acutely, made a world for us: "And when she sang, the sea . . . became the self that was her song." At least for her: "there never was a world for her / Except the one she sang and, singing, made." And yet she made the world for us as well. When the singing ended, the lights of the anchored fishing boats "Mastered the night and portioned out the sea . . . / Arranging, deepening, enchanting night." Like the pillars of Nature's temple, the sea speaks words which the maker orders, words of the sea and words of the sky, "And of ourselves and of our origins, / In ghostlier demarcations, keener sounds."

In Ashbery's "The Painter," a man, unnamed as well, sits "between the sea and the buildings," between nature and culture, painting the sea's portrait. Or rather, waiting for such a portrait to paint itself. The poem's repeating end words indicate its concerns quite clearly: "portrait," "subject," "canvas," "brush," "prayer," and "buildings." We are in the realm of the relations among representation, the making subject, that subject's subject matter, his medium and materials, his hopes, and the concrete manifestations of his cultural context, which both restrain and make possible.

The painter expects the sea, limbless and eyeless though it is, to seize a brush and "Plaster its own portrait on the canvas." Having planted himself between nature and artifice, he expects nature to produce its own art, until those on the other end of the spectrum, the people who live in the buildings, remind him that art is not life. "Try using the brush / As a means to an end." The sea is too vast a subject, too unwilling to subject itself to a painter's moods or prayers. But he wants "nature, not art, [to] usurp the canvas." Attempting to take their advice, he paints his wife, but makes her "vast, like ruined buildings," like the sea, "As if, forgetting itself, the portrait / Had expressed itself without a brush." A good try, at least: there is something on the canvas, however boundless. "Slightly encouraged," he tries again, dipping his brush into the sea as if for a benediction. He no longer expects the sea to paint its own portrait; now his soul will do so, wrecking the canvas (Picasso called his pictures "a sum of destructions," and such a demolition of what is can often be crucial to the creation of what might be). The sea is his subject once again, but it will never subject itself to him. The task is too large; he is crucified by his subject, "Too exhausted even to lift his brush," and mocked by other artists more securely ensconced in the realm of culture, the land of artifice. The sea will never sit for a portrait. His painting is only a self-portrait, or so others declare, and it is blank (he seems to have no self of his own): "Finally all indications of a subject / Began to fade, leaving the canvas / Perfectly white. He put down the brush." Unlike Stevens's singer by the side of the sea, he does not seem to realize that his portrait of the sea must be his own and made by him.

"*Le livre est sur la table*" is also in dialogue with "The Idea of Order at Key West." Knowing that beauty exists only by reason of absence or oddity, "deprivation or logic / Or strange position," in this poem "We can only imagine a world in which a woman / Walks and wears her hair and knows / All that she does not know." Which is to say either that in a world in which "beauty, resonance, integrity" are so difficult of access our only recourse is to imagine this woman who knows what she does not know (itself a notion with a double sense), or that such a world of knowing unknownness can only be imagined, being so far from our own. This woman might well be walking by the sea, singing the sea, before she goes into the house, "from which the wailing starts," a kind of song after all, however mournful and cacophonous. And then there is a young man placing a bird-house "Against the blue sea": "He walks away and it remains," a token of human presence and also a liminal object between the natural and artificial, man-made but housing natural creatures. Meanwhile, other men appear who live in other kinds of boxes; "The sea protects them like a wall." But a wall against what? A woman appears again, or the representation of a woman, a line-drawing worshipped by the gods, "in the shadow of the sea / Which goes on writing." While Stevens's woman sings the sea in singing herself, this sea writes itself. "Did all secrets vanish when / The woman left?" can ask either whether all secrets have disappeared in her absence or whether all secrets have been revealed in that absence. I suspect it asks both at once: there are indeed collisions, of land and water, of mind and world, of art and nature, "communications on the shore." The book is on the table, and we are reading it.

"The Instruction Manual": how mundane, how earth-bound, yet how necessary if one is in need of instruction. And when is one not in need of instruction, if not on the uses of a new metal then perhaps on the uses of one's own mettle, new or old, or even where such mettle might be found? One place it might be found is in the imagination, which as Stevens points out discloses but does not invent. Someone is always in need of instruction somewhere, and someone else must provide that instruction, write that manual. But he would rather look out the window at the people walking up and down the streets with an inner peace he knows they possess because they are not him, because they are so far away from him, because they are not tasked with the task of instruction. He begins to dream, he rests his elbows on the desk and leans a little out the window, and he sees a city indeed, not the unnamed city in which he is busily not writing an instruction manual, but "dim Guadalajara! City of rose-colored flowers! / City I wanted most to see, and most did not see, in Mexico!" But, "under the press of having to write the instruction manual," he sees it now, or fancies he does, the public square with a band playing Rimsky-Korsakov's *Scheherazade* on the elaborate little bandstand, the flower girls in their rose-and-striped dresses, the women in green in little white booths serving green and yellow fruit. In poet and critic Catherine Imbriglio's fine phrase, the speaker is "a sort of voyeur in the land of his own imagination."

Poetry is an art of "as if," a way of "what if," and "The Instruction Manual" presents us with a vivid picture of what has not been seen at all, of what exists only in the imagination of the speaker, who does not (or not yet, not in this poem) write the manual of the title, but does indeed write something, a manual of sorts, this guide to a Guadalajara of the mind, or at least of one mind. It is as if we too have been to Guadalajara in our minds. What if we had been to Guadalajara? Here are some things we might have seen. More broadly, here are some things one might see when one looks with the mind's eye.

The poem is indeed an instruction manual: in those moments of vacant labor, in those moments when the world is too much with us, near or far, we can take refuge in the mind, can travel anywhere in the globe while still chained to our desks. The poem will show us how to imagine this other place in greater detail than we have ever noticed anything more immediately around us, certainly than we have seen or cared to see the office where the instruction manual still waits to be written, its potential author having traveled elsewhere.

Though by the poem's end, his journey's end, he must turn his attention away from the Guadalajara he has written for us and back to the instruction manual which was his motive for imagining this mental Guadalajara in the first place—"What more is there to do, except stay? And that we cannot do"—the speaker (the maker, the poet) has at least earned himself a respite from what is, and has taken us on a trip to a place we have never been and never will go again, since it is not Guadalajara we have visited, but rather "Guadalajara."

Brief Notes on Celan, Difficulty, and Meaning

Poetry offers many other pleasures and possibilities than meaning. But meaning is one of the possibilities that poetry offers, a not inconsiderable one, and poetry cannot help but offer it. "Meaning is present even in the statement that there is no meaning" (Adorno 154). That possibility cannot be evaded or denied, because poems, even the most aleatory or rigorously procedural, are products of human intention, including the intention to write an aleatory or procedural poem from which individual intention will be evacuated. (One could put this as "I intend not to intend." Or, more precisely but more verbosely, "I intend that my intention will not determine the outcome of the process of writing this poem.")

A throw of the dice will never abolish chance, as Mallarmé wrote, but it is the human hand that tosses the dice and the human mind and will that decide the meaning of that dice toss's outcome. As human productions, aesthetic objects are infused with what Kant calls purposiveness, though aesthetic purposiveness is a paradoxical purpose without a purpose, without, that is, any practical or instrumental aim. As Adorno writes in *Aesthetic Theory,* "In art, the true point of reference continues to be the subject" (63).

To assert, as some do, that Paul Celan was not interested in meaning or communication is to evade or shrug off the work of actually reading his poems: it is to trivialize those poems, to erase their working at and working through. Celan, who insisted that his poetry was "absolutely not hermetic" (*Ganz und gar nicht hermetisch,* as he inscribed in Michael Hamburger's copy of *Die*

Niemandrose), often questioned the possibility of saying, but never its value or its necessity. As Michael Hamburger writes, "If Celan had set out to write hermetic poems, his work would be less difficult than it is, because it would not require us to make the kind of sense of it that we know it can yield" ("Introduction," *Poems of Paul Celan* xxv). Celan did not set out to babble in or play with language. Celan's work is not "experimentation" in the sense which Adorno condemns as "chimerical and specious: on the one hand [the most recent experimental procedures] are tinged with subjectivity; on the other they suppose that art can divest itself of its subjectivity through experimentation, becoming at last what it has always pretended to be, namely a being in itself free of appearance" (36).

Celan writes in his 1958 speech on receiving the city of Bremen's literature prize that "in this language [he is referring specifically to the German language, stained and scarred by the enormity of the Holocaust] I have sought . . . to write poems so as to speak, to orient myself, to find out where I was and where I was meant to go, to sketch out reality for myself." As he writes later in the same speech: "A poem, as a manifestation of language and thus essentially dialogue, can be a message in a bottle sent out in the—not always greatly hopeful—belief that somewhere and sometime it could wash up on land, on heartland perhaps. Poems in this sense too are underway: they are making toward something." Despite and by means of their difficulty, Celan's poems seek, desperately and perhaps hopelessly, communication, contact, connection, even if not in the here and now: as he writes in the poem "Threadsuns" ("Fadensonnen"), "there are / still songs to sing beyond / humankind." There is almost always a "you" to whom his poems are directed, to whom his poems try to speak. "Without a You," the brainless, Youless hordes rush in, with their meaningless words. The message may not reach anyone, and if it does, it may not be apprehended, comprehended. But the possibility, the likelihood even, of failure makes more acute the will to attempt contact, to try to make a connection.

In 1961's "The Meridian" (*Selected Poems and Prose of Paul Celan*), his longest and best-known piece of prose, Celan writes:

> The poem wants to reach an Other, it needs this Other, it needs an over-against. It seeks it out, speaks toward it.
>
> For the poem making toward an Other, each thing, each human being is a form of this Other.
>
> The attentiveness a poem devotes to all it encounters, with its sharper sense of detail, outline, structure, color, but also of "quiverings" and "intimations"—all this, I think, is not attained by an eye vying (or conniving) with constantly more perfect instruments. Rather, it is a conversation that stays mindful of all our dates. (409–10)

> A poem—under what conditions!—becomes the poem of someone (ever yet) perceiving, facing phenomena, questioning and addressing those phenomena; it becomes conversation—often despairing conversation. (410)

Far from disdaining meaning, reference, or communication, Celan is the textbook example of the modern poet who, in Eliot's description of his activity, "must become more and more comprehensive, more allusive, more indirect, in order to force, to dislocate if necessary, language into his meaning" ("The Metaphysical Poets," *Selected Prose of T. S. Eliot,* 65). He must wrestle with, deform, and be deformed by language (the angel from the struggle with which one rises lamed but blessed, renamed) to make it mean anew, to make it mean again. In particular, Celan attempts to speak the unspeakable, to redeem by reinventing (and rebuking) a language permanently tainted by the incommensurable horror of the Shoah. He seeks to remove "the veil / over road-weary / mouths" ("White noise, bundled" / "Weissgeräusche"), the mouths which can no longer speak and the mouths which, despairing and overwhelmed, will no longer speak.

Even when one doesn't derive an immediately paraphrasable statement from his poems, one feels the urgency, one is struck by the vivid imagery, immersed in the worldscapes Celan conjures. The poems never seem to be about nothing, though they sometimes brood on the void of Nothing. They are always, in the words of "Wet from the world" ("Die abgewrackten Tabus"), "pursuing / meaning, fleeing / meaning": fleeing the easy meanings, the always-on-offer lies masquerading as truth, seeking a deeper, more hard-won meaning.

Celan was passionately committed to meaning, reference, and communication. He often asked himself "How assemble meaning?" (every poem of his asks that question), but never "Why assemble meaning?" As Michael Hamburger writes in *The Truth of Poetry*, "This artistic purism is content with nothing less than 'raids on the inarticulate.' It would be impertinent to speculate how much of Celan's later practice is due to extreme experience, how much to the artistic rigor of an unrepentant modernist. What is certain about Celan's later poems is that they explore the limits of language and the limits of consciousness, groping their way towards a communion that may be religious or mystical, since their starting-point is total solitude and their destination [is 'beyond humankind']" (295).

WORKS CITED

Adorno, Theodor W. *Aesthetic Theory.* Trans. C. Lenhardt. New York: Routledge and Kegan Paul, 1984.

Celan, Paul. *Poems of Paul Celan.* Trans. Michael Hamburger. New York: Persea Books, 1972.

Celan, Paul. *Selected Poems and Prose of Paul Celan.* Trans. John Felstiner. New York: W. W. Norton, 2001.

Eliot, T. S. *Selected Prose of T. S. Eliot.* Ed. Frank Kermode. New York: Farrar, Straus and Giroux, 1975.

Hamburger, Michael. *The Truth of Poetry: Tensions in Modern Poetry from Baudelaire to the Nineteen-Sixties.* New York: Harcourt Brace and World, 1972.

Art and Society

A Few Words on Wilfred Owen

Wilfred Owen, whom World War I both brought to maturity as a poet and killed, is not much read or thought about these days. But his poetry of the sorrow and pity of war, his astringent eye for the lies of patriotic self-sacrifice (that is, the demands that others sacrifice themselves), seem very appropriate to our new world order of seemingly permanent war. Yeats dismissed his work as "all blood, dirt & sucked sugar stick," that is, as too base, and yet it is that baseness, that groundedness, that makes Owens's poetry live for us today.

I am impressed by how much of an experimental poet Owen was. "Dulce et Decorum Est," which I will discuss in detail, is among other things a formal and thematic commentary on the conventions of the sonnet. The sonnet, which traditionally engages an idealized vision of the world, here is turned to the rather gruesome description of painful, pointless death, becoming a kind of anti-sonnet engaging an anti-ideal. I'd like to look at some of the ways the poem uses and refuses the conventions of the sonnet form, and the ways that its formal distortions and dislocations enact and embody the distortion and dislocation of human lives and human values enacted by war, in which men sleepwalk toward death (their "distant rest") for the profit of those who will never see a battlefield.

Dulce et Decorum Est

Bent double, like old beggars under sacks,
Knock-kneed, coughing like hags, we cursed through sludge,
Till on the haunting flares we turned our backs
And towards our distant rest began to trudge.
Men marched asleep. Many had lost their boots
But limped on, blood-shod. All went lame; all blind;

Drunk with fatigue; deaf even to the hoots
Of tired, outstripped Five-Nines that dropped behind.

Gas! GAS! Quick, boys!—An ecstasy of fumbling
Fitting the clumsy helmets just in time;
But someone still was yelling out and stumbling,
And flound'ring like a man in fire or lime . . .
Dim, through the misty panes and thick green light,
As under a green sea, I saw him drowning.

In all my dreams, before my helpless sight,
He plunges at me, guttering, choking, drowning.

If in some smothering dreams you too could pace
Behind the wagon that we flung him in,
And watch the white eyes writhing in his face,
His hanging face, like a devil's sick of sin;
If you could hear, at every jolt, the blood

Come gargling from the froth-corrupted lungs
Obscene as cancer, bitter as the cud
Of vile, incurable sores on innocent tongues,—
My friend, you would not tell with such high zest
To children ardent for some desperate glory,
The old Lie: Dulce et decorum est
Pro patria mori.

"Dulce et Decorum Est" can be read both as two sonnets, in which the second half (the second sonnet) answers the first half (the first sonnet), and as a double sonnet of twenty-eight lines in which the break between the two sections (the past and the present) constitutes the volte or turn, dividing the piece in half instead of the traditional Petrarchan proportion of eight to six. The poem also follows the traditional thematic pattern of the Petrarchan sonnet, in which the first part sets out a problem or situation and the second part sets out a solution or response. Here, we have the brutal narrative of the first half, followed by the recollection and moral reflection of the second half. The poem can also be read as a truncated sonnet sequence, as if to say "I can't do that sort of thing anymore, not after what I've seen."

The formal adventurism of "Dulce et Decorum Est" is evident in its combination of the contours of a sonnet (the first fourteen lines are even set typographically as a Petrarchan sonnet) with a quatrain rhyme structure. Owen also plays with formal expectations by concealing the quatrain rhyme scheme typographically, even breaking stanzas in the middle of quatrains. And he plays that quatrain rhyme scheme against the sonnet thematic/narrative structure in a kind of poetic counterpoint.

Read as a sonnet, the first half of the poem combines the octave of a Shakespearean sonnet with a more improvisational sestet in which the end words of two lines, "light" and "drowning," don't rhyme at all. We don't return to the rhyme until we come to the word "sight" at the end of the first line of the second sonnet, and it is indeed that "thick green light" (of the poison gas) that makes possible and leads to the speaker's "helpless sight" that still haunts his dreams, the sight of his fellow soldier "choking, drowning." This is immediately followed by the reappearance of the word "drowning," to emphasize that the speaker's comrade is, for him, perpetually drowning. That the rhymes cut across the boundaries of the poem's two halves (they're part of a single quatrain, yet also the end and the beginning of the two halves of the poem) emphasizes the presence of the past horror in the present moment. The repetition of the word "drowning," an ironically perfect rhyme, between lines in the poem's two halves plays out both connection (the identity of the sounds and of the experience the sounds represent) and disconnection (since the experience is of the death of another, which by definition cannot be shared). By beginning the poem's second half with two lines that rhyme with nothing else in that half of the poem (that is, in that sonnet), the poem enacts the psychic and spiritual disorder which is its theme. A similar effect occurs at the end of the poem, when the pentameter line is truncated (like the life of that fallen soldier and so many of his comrades) down to a trimeter. The poem is whittled down to death, ending on the Latin word "mori," to die.

The first half or first sonnet of the poem also has a turn or volte at the expected moment in a traditional sonnet, at the stanza break after the octave, when the poem switches from a more objective description of the soldiers' situation (though a description that is also heavily symbolic, as the soldiers trudge unconsciously toward their "distant rest," that is, toward their deaths) to an immersion in the situation signaled by the eruption of direct speech into the poem: "Gas! GAS! Quick, boys!" At this point the poem also shifts from a description of group's experience to a focus on that of an individual, the one "still yelling out and stumbling" who didn't get his gas mask on in time. It also shifts to the speaker's individual experience of watching this man die: "I saw him drowning." This ending on the word "drowning" echoes the end of the poem's second half and thus of the poem as a whole. Both halves end in death, like the experience of which the poem speaks, like the war it commemorates and condemns.

The poem's second half begins with the repetition of this individual experience:

> In all my dreams, before all my helpless sight,
> He plunges at me, guttering, choking, drowning.

But then it turns to direct address and chastisement of the reader and thus of the society of which the reader is a part, which expects art to be uplifting and patriotic and death to be noble and glorious. It's sweet and proper to die for one's country. This poem exposes the truth of that "old Lie." In that regard, it seems very much a poem of our moment.

Adorno, Celan, and the Possibility of Poetry

Theodor Adorno and Paul Celan appear almost as mirror images. Adorno's work might be said to be the theory of which Celan's poetry is the practice. Or, not to prioritize theory over praxis, it might equally be said that Celan's poetry, addressing and enacting what Michael Hamburger in *The Truth of Poetry* calls "the question of what can still be said or no longer said in poetry" (290), is the practice of which Adorno's work is the theory. Celan and Samuel Beckett are the only two contemporary writers Adorno discusses in his posthumously published *Aesthetic Theory*. As Celan's biographer John Felstiner notes, "Finding such stringency [in their work], Theodor Adorno thought Celan the only authentic postwar writer to stand with Samuel Beckett and made copious notes in his copy of Celan's *Sprachgitter* [Speech Grille]" (107).

Adorno wrote that Celan was "the greatest exponent of hermetic poetry in present-day Germany." However, in the same discussion, Adorno pointed out that Celan's poems "give rise to the question of just how hermetic they are," because in them "the experiential content of the hermetic is the opposite of what it used to be" (*Aesthetic Theory* 443, 444). As Celan insisted, his poetry is not at all hermetic (*ganz und gar nicht hermetisch*), certainly not in the traditional sense of the escapist religion of art. "His poetry is permeated by the shame of art in the face of suffering that escapes both experience and sublimation" (Adorno, *Aesthetic Theory* 444). Rather than turning away or averting its gaze from historical suffering, Celan's poetry faces it with its own Medusa gaze.

Allen Grossman says in an interview in the *Harvard Advocate* that "a strong poetry would be a poetry that discerns and finds a poetically adequate means of bringing to mind the catastrophe of history." This bringing to consciousness of the catastrophe (Walter Benjamin's storm of history) which both forms and deforms us is one of the many tasks that Celan's poetry sets itself.

Adorno's dictum on poetry after Auschwitz has become famous, or infamous. On the last page of his essay "Cultural Criticism and Society," written in 1949, first published in 1951, and collected in *Prisms* in 1955, he writes that "even the most extreme consciousness of doom threatens to degenerate into idle chatter. Cultural criticism finds itself faced with the final stage of the dialectic of culture and barbarism. To write poetry after Auschwitz is barbaric. And this corrodes even the knowledge of why it has become impossible to write poetry today" (*Prisms* 34).

Despite Adorno's high opinion of Celan's work, Celan believed that Adorno's stricture was directed against his poem "Todesfuge" (Death Fugue) (which Hamburger calls "perhaps the only decisive proof that poems could be written not only after Auschwitz but about the cold horrors perpetrated there" [290]), although Felstiner points out that Adorno was probably not aware of the poem at the time (139). It wasn't published in Germany until 1952, when Celan's collection *Mohn und Gedächtnis* (*Poppy and Memory*) appeared.

Adorno revisited and considerably modified his position on the possibility of poetry after Auschwitz in his 1961 essay "Engagement," collected in the posthumous two-volume collection *Notes to Literature.* In the edited collection *Aesthetics and Politics,* published by New Left Books in 1977 and currently available from Verso, this essay is translated as "Commitment." It is this translation from which I quote here. The essay is primarily a polemic against Brecht's and Sartre's demands for a committed literature or a *littérature engagée.* In it Adorno reaffirms his original statement about the barbarism of writing poetry after Auschwitz while also complicating it in such a way as not only to allow literature's continued existence but to require it. This can be considered an Hegelian sublation of his original dictum, canceling it out while raising it up to a higher, more complex level.

In "Commitment," Adorno asserts that "I have no wish to soften the saying that to write lyric poetry after Auschwitz is barbaric; it expresses in negative form the impulse which inspires committed literature. The question asked by a character in Sartre's play *Morts Sans Sepulture* [translated as *Men without Shadows*], 'Is there any meaning in life when men exist who beat people until the bones break in their bodies?', is also the question of whether any art now has the right to exist; whether intellectual regression is not inherent in the concept of committed literature because of the regression of society." However, Adorno goes on to admit that German poet and polemicist Hans Magnus "Enzensberger's retort also remains true, that literature must resist this verdict, in other words, be such that its mere existence after Auschwitz is not a surrender to cynicism. Its own situation is one of paradox, not merely the problem of how to react to it. The abundance of real suffering tolerates no forgetting; Pascal's theological saying, *On ne doit plus dormer* [One should not sleep anymore], must be secularized. Yet this suffering, what Hegel called consciousness of adversity, also demands the continuing existence of art while it prohibits it; it is now virtually in art alone that suffering can still find its own voice, consolation, without immediately being betrayed by it. The most important artists of the age have realized this. The uncompromising radicalism of their works, the very features defamed as formalism, give them a terrifying power, absent from helpless poems to the victims of our time" (*Aesthetics and Politics* 188–89).

Adorno goes on to discuss Arnold Schoenberg's 1948 composition *A Survivor from Warsaw,* which evokes the destruction of the Warsaw Ghetto, pointing out the inevitable tension between artistic stylization and the claims of justice, two incompatible necessities. So this point, at which he reaffirms his statement, is also the point at which he turns that statement on its head. (By selectively quoting so as to leave out the substance of Adorno's statement, Felstiner distorts Adorno's meaning in this passage, framing it as an implicit criticism of Celan.)

Thus, Adorno's complication of his stricture against writing poetry after Auschwitz not only makes room for art, but specifically makes room for the kind of art that Celan made. In *Aesthetic Theory,* Adorno goes so far as to write that, far from being barbaric after the horrors of the Holocaust, "art may be the only remaining medium of truth in an age of incomprehensible suffering. As the real world grows dark, the irrationality of art is becoming rational, especially at a time when art is radically tenebrous itself" (27).

John Felstiner's biography *Paul Celan: Poet, Survivor, Jew* is almost infinitely useful in identifying, describing, and untangling the complex fabric of Celan's poetry. But it is also a bit tendentious. Felstiner identifies too much with Celan's paranoia and sense of isolation—he wants to construct Celan as alone and lonely, perpetually misunderstood, persecuted, and unappreciated. There was enough genuine pain in Celan's life (both his parents died in the Holocaust and he drowned himself in the River Seine) without the need to manufacture it for the sake of narrative melodrama.

Felstiner seems to harbor an active animus toward Adorno. He calls Celan's reaction to the news of Adorno's death—"I am struck, dismayed"—"not quite his strongest words" (263), and mentions a slighting reference Celan made to Adorno, "who I thought was a Jew," referring to Adorno's adoption of his Catholic mother's maiden name rather than his Jewish father's surname, Wiesengrund (139).

In *Negative Dialectics,* Adorno writes that "perennial suffering has as much right to expression as the tortured have to scream; hence it may have been wrong to say that after Auschwitz you could no longer write poems" (362). After describing this passage as a recantation of Adorno's earlier dictum (which is a simplification to say the least), Felstiner comments rather snippily that "this came rather late, as Celan's verse had exercised that right for some time" (232).

Moreover, Felstiner crucially fails to cite the rest of the passage in question: "But it is not wrong to ask the less cultural question whether after Auschwitz you can go on living—especially whether one who escaped by accident, one who by rights should have been killed, may go on living. His mere survival calls for the coldness, the basic principle of bourgeois subjectivity, without which there could have been no Auschwitz; this is the drastic guilt of him who was spared. [This sentence can be read as a highly particularized and even personalized example of the paradox of the dialectic of enlightenment, in which the logic of instrumental reason leads enlightenment into its opposites, domination and barbarism.] By way of atonement he will be plagued by dreams such as that he is no longer living at all, that he was sent to the ovens in 1944 and [that] his whole existence since then has been imaginary, an emanation of the insane wish of a man killed twenty years earlier" (362–63).

Adorno is obviously writing here of himself and his own survivor guilt at having escaped the fate that overcame so many millions of other Jews, but this description also sounds like Celan to the letter. It is to the letter that both Adorno and Celan are faithful, and by the letter that each wrote.

WORKS CITED

Adorno, Theodor W. *Aesthetic Theory.* Trans. C. Lenhardt. New York: Routledge and Kegan Paul, 1984.

Adorno, Theodor W. "Commitment." *Aesthetics and Politics.* Trans. and ed. Ronald Taylor. London: Verso, 1980.

Adorno, Theodor W. *Negative Dialectics.* Trans. E. B. Ashton. New York: Continuum, 1973.

Adorno, Theodor W. *Prisms.* Trans. Samuel Weber and Shierry Weber. Cambridge: MIT Press, 1981.

Felstiner, John. *Paul Celan: Poet, Survivor, Jew.* New Haven: Yale University Press, 1995.

Hamburger, Michael. *The Truth of Poetry: Tensions in Modern Poetry from Baudelaire to the Nineteen-Sixties.* New York: Harcourt Brace and World, 1972.

Caliban to the Audience
The Tempest *as Colonialist and Anti-Colonialist Text*

Stephen Greenblatt, writing with an enviable critical certainty, informs us that "Shakespeare's plays are centrally and repeatedly concerned with the production and containment of subversion and disorder" (29). The plays summon up challenges to the social and symbolic order so that these challenges may then be contained by means of various ideological mystifications. At the same time, the very necessity of this repeated gesture of containment enacts the possibility (indeed, the inevitability) of its own failure. Ideology is, after all, the imaginary resolution of real contradictions. The challenges these plays attempt to master—challenges to the patriarchal family, to patrilineal succession, to the subordination of the "base-born" to the "noble" and of women to men—were and are not reducible to dangers within discourse: as the long history of, on the one hand, wars of dynastic succession and, on the other hand, peasant rebellions and uprisings illustrates.

The Tempest, if read in relation to the (evolving and inconsistent) English colonial project in the New World, lays out the real contradictions it will imaginarily (that is, ideologically) resolve with exemplary clarity. The play "serves as a limit text in which the characteristic operations of colonialist discourse may be discerned—as an instrument of exploitation, a register of beleaguerment and a site of radical ambivalence. These operations produce strategies and stereotypes which seek to impose and efface colonial power; in this text they are also driven into contradiction and disruption" (Brown 68). My emphasis is on the ways in which the play disrupts the incipient English colonial project by unmasking and disrupting the smooth operation of its mechanics. Whether the play's rather edifying laying bare of the device (to cite the Russian Formalist Viktor Shklovsky's phrase) of imperialism would in its own time have been read as a critique of these mechanisms' mendacity or merely as confirmation of their cleverness and efficacy is not a question I, or anyone now living, can answer. It is also a question that, as Greenblatt indicates in his discussion of Thomas Harriot's *A Brief and True Report of the New Found Land of Virginia,* need not be taken to have had an unequivocal answer even at the time of the play's original performance, especially given what Paul Brown calls the ambivalences and contradictions of the colonial discourse itself.

Thomas Cartelli argues that the play's "capacity to make a significant intervention in the formation of colonialist discourse and in the development of colonialist practices . . . was inhibited from the start by the play's generic resemblances to and rehearsals of contemporary reports of colonial encounters. Indeed, the play's very participation in this formative moment through the medium of Prospero's expropriation of Caliban's island, and his act's perceived consistency with the colonial ventures of a [Sir Walter] Raleigh and the partisan writings of the Hakluyts, can be said to have condemned the play to participate also in that discourse's evolution and eventual rigidification in the imperial moment of Britain's colonization of Africa" (108–9). However, Cartelli's subsequent discussion of postcolonial and anti-imperialist appropriations of the play demonstrates that it need not be read, or taken to be readable, so univocally.

"*The Tempest* is not simply a reflection of colonialist practices but an intervention in an ambivalent and even contradictory discourse. This intervention takes the form of a powerful and pleasurable narrative which seeks at once to harmonize disjunction, to transcend irreconcilable contradictions and to mystify the political conditions which demand colonialist discourse. Yet the narrative ultimately fails to deliver that containment and instead may be seen to foreground precisely those problems which it works to efface or overcome" (Brown 48). By allowing the "Other" to speak and make his case, if only in the ostensible master's language, the text permits the undermining of the colonialist discourse it not only participates in but in some ways inaugurates. Indeed, the very fact of Caliban's mastery of the master's tongue "ensures that its interpellation of him as simply savage, 'a born devil, on whose nature / Nurture can never stick' (IV.i.188–9) is inadequate. Paradoxically, it is the eloquent power of civility which allows him to know [and to speak] his own meaning, offering him a site of resistance even as civility's coercive capacities finally reduce him to silence" (Brown 62–63). That "civility" is thus shown to require coercion to produce the Other's silence may be taken as an indication of the play's resistance to its own apparent ideological project. Whether the text actively works to undermine colonialist discourse or merely "permits" a reading that produces such subversion is an open question.

Whether *The Tempest* is "about" the English colonial project (then only in its incipient stages: much of Greenblatt's discussion seems much more applicable to the Spanish colonial project, by then well under way) in any direct manner is another question without an unequivocal answer, as the long history of critical controversy on this point (a history I will not engage here) illustrates. Whatever its surface engagements with the dynastic affairs of the ruling houses of various Italian petty states, the play is very much informed by the anxieties and excitations of the English encounter with the Western hemisphere and the various peoples inhabiting that world much less "New" to them. These anxieties, along with those relating to dynasty and proper kinship relations, are within its confines worked through in a displaced and condensed manner much like that of the Freudian dream-work. (Paul Brown has explored this analogy, and the related concept of the play's political unconscious, in much greater detail in the essay from which I have quoted so extensively.)

"*The Tempest*'s status as a privileged text in the history of colonialist discourse" (Cartelli 110) seems neither coincidental nor accidental. I am struck by the constant parallel the play asks the reader or viewer to draw between the relations of Prospero to Caliban and Ariel and the relations of the English colonists to the "Indians" of the "New World," even down to such details as the remarkable resemblance of the water with berries in it Prospero gives Caliban to the liquor the Europeans introduced to the "natives." It furthermore proleptically figures many aspects of the European colonial project in its full exfoliation, particularly that project's "convergence of assumed high-mindedness with brutality" (Cartelli 110).

My discussion focuses on the figure of Caliban, reading the play from what can only be my version of his perspective. Caliban and Ariel can together be read as a double vision of the indigenous peoples of the "New World," a vision (simultaneously wishful and prophetic) in which their threat to the colonial project has been securely neutralized at the very moment of being acknowledged.

Ariel is a figure of the "good" native who, though he may at times complain of his servitude, still accedes to it. To put it crudely, he is the hard-working darky who loves and is loved by his master, and performs his imposed labors with good cheer. He accepts (though under explicit threat) Prospero's version of his enslavement as a form of liberation:

> . . . Thou best know'st
> What torment I did find thee in; . . .
> . . . It was mine art,
> When I arriv'd and heard thee, that made gape
> The pine, and let thee out.
> Ariel: I thank thee, master. (I.ii.286–87, 291–93)

Except in its literalization as entrapment in a tree, Prospero's account of the brute state of nature from which he has ostensibly rescued Ariel closely resembles European justifications of their presence in and domination of the *soi-disant* New World. "Ariel is, paradoxically, bound in service by this constant reminder of Prospero's gift of freedom to him, in releasing him from imprisonment in a tree. That bondage is reinforced by both a promise to repeat the act of release when a period of servitude has expired and a promise to repeat the act of incarceration should service not be forthcoming" (Brown 60). In one of the play's many imaginary resolutions, Ariel is manumitted for having served so faithfully and so well: he is set free as a reward for not having attempted to free himself.

By contrast, Caliban is a figure of the bad, "rebellious" native.

In striking contrast to Ariel, Caliban is in Prospero's version of things denied his very indigenousness, though whatever Sycorax's provenance her son was born on the island. It is Caliban who insists on his "illegitimate" rights to the land Prospero has "discovered":

> This island's mine by Sycorax my mother,
> Which thou tak'st from me. (I.ii.331–32)

Prospero's implicit counter-assertion that before his arrival "this island / . . . [was] not honor'd with / A human shape," except, and merely parenthetically, for Caliban, who does not, in Prospero's view, quite count:

> Dull thing, I say so; he, that Caliban
> Whom I now keep in service. (I.ii.284–85)

is hardly different in kind from the pretensions of the European invaders in nominating two well-populated continents as a "New World," and their own.

Caliban's claim to the island is made in specifically dynastic terms, and thus both parallels and rivals Prospero's to Milan and Ferdinand's to Naples. Caliban and Prospero share the status of rulers dispossessed of their demesnes by false-dealing. For that matter, Caliban, as a deposed king, actually ranks higher than Prospero does as a deposed duke. Caliban's supposed attempted rape of Miranda, besides serving as an example of the way in which "things of darkness" are regularly accused of provoking their own enslavement or worse (the rape attempt is, after all, the reason Prospero gives for Caliban's servitude), mirrors, as in a glass, darkly, Ferdinand's determinedly chaste (determined by Prospero, that is) courtship of Miranda later in the play. Caliban's aborted union with Miranda represents the possibility of a dynastic alliance of the island with Milan. This possibility, of equality between two forces not yet definitely marked as colonized and colonizer, is one Prospero rejects in favor of subjugating the island to his power and thus to that of Europe as figured by Milan. "What appears to disturb Prospero even more than Caliban's foiled attempt to violate Miranda's honor is Caliban's insistence on recalling his former sovereignty, his repeated effort to lay claim to a history and inheritance which imply a state of equality at odds with his assigned status as slave. It is in the face of Caliban's assertion that 'I am all the subjects that you have, / Which first was my own King' [*sic*] (and not to any denial of his attempt to rape Miranda) that Prospero responds, 'Thou most lying slave, / Whom stripes may move, not kindness' (I.ii.343–44, 346–47)" (Cartelli 110).

In this light, Caliban's status as only son of the island's previous ruler, with a duty to perpetuate his line by producing an heir, becomes more clear, and his exclamation that

> . . . I had peopled else
> This isle with Calibans. (I.ii.350–51)

is seen as more than the expression of mere bestial lust Prospero insists it be taken as, but rather as an expression of the dynastic imperative which Caliban and Prospero share. What also becomes clear from this viewpoint is Ferdinand's status as the approved, white European version of Caliban. Ferdinand is the one with a royal claim (and thus, in a rigidly hierarchical society in which one's purchase on humanity is defined by one's status, a claim to full personhood) acknowledged and respected within the European power system. Just as Caliban sees and desires Miranda, and specifically sees her as a mother of potential heirs, so Ferdinand sees and desires Miranda as a potential Queen of Naples: he'll people Naples with Ferdinands. That Prospero both rejects Caliban's claim to kingship and knows Ferdinand's claim to (present though not future) kingship to be an illusion (since Ferdinand's father, Alonso, King of Naples, is not in fact dead, though Ferdinand thinks that he is) points up the parallel further, because both the false nature of Caliban's claim and the illusory nature of Ferdinand's are Prospero's doing.

The implicitly deceitful friendliness Caliban accuses Prospero of practicing on the latter's first arrival on the island (in a condition, like that of the first colonial settlers in the "New World," of great vulnerability and need) seems remarkably like that of the first Virginia colonists. Whatever counter-argument Prospero presents, Caliban clearly indicates that Prospero used him to learn the lay of the (is)land, then enslaved him when Prospero's position of superiority was secured:

> . . . When thou cam'st first,
> Thou strok'st me and made much of me, wouldst give me
> Water with berries in't . . .
> . . . and then I lov'd thee
> And show'd thee all the qualities o' th' isle,
> The fresh springs, brine-pits, barren place and fertile.
> Curs'd be I that did so! . . .
> For I am all the subjects that you have,
> Which first was mine own king; and here you sty me
> In this hard rock, whiles you do keep from me
> The rest o' th' island. (I.ii.332–34, 336–39, 341–44)

That part of Prospero's response to his "lying slave" is the assertion to "have us'd thee / (Filth as thou art) with human care" (I.ii.345–46) does not support the justice of his claim, especially given the ambiguity of the word "use."

The English colonists' use of religion and superior technology appearing as magic to manipulate the natives is analogous to Prospero's use of magic gotten from books to subdue and render usefully obedient Caliban and Ariel. ("Bible," in case we needed any reminding, means "book.") "If we remember that, like virtually all sixteenth-century Europeans in the New World, the English resisted or were incapable of provisioning themselves and were in consequence dependent upon the Indians for food, we may grasp the central importance for the colonists of this dawning Indian fear of the Christian God. As Machiavelli understood, physical compulsion is essential but never sufficient; the survival of the rulers depends upon a supplement of coercive belief" (Greenblatt 23). As Caliban says, prompted as much by Prospero's repeated insistence on his power to compel his "slave" to "make our fire, / Fetch in our wood, and [serve] in office / That profit us" (I.ii.311–13) as by the pinches and frights and trifles that Prospero sets on him when he expresses insubordination,

> . . . His art is of such power
> It would control my dam's god Setebos,
> And make a vassal of him. (I.ii.371–73)

Greenblatt describes the English manipulating such occasions as the spread of epidemic disease as demonstrations of the superior strength of their God versus the gods of the Indians (Setebos, we should recall, was the English version of the name of a Patagonian god); similarly, Prospero manipulates his control over elves and "demi-puppets" to impose such a belief on Caliban. "The key to this imposition . . . is the coercive power of religious belief, and the source of this power is the impression made by advanced technology [in this case, Prospero's books] upon a 'backward' people" (Greenblatt 24). Indeed, the lesson of the Stephano-Trinculo sub-plot (besides that European social inferiors who attempt to rise above their station will always and easily be put back in their rightful places) is that Caliban has taken the wrong white men (i.e., commoners) to be gods: "Caliban misrecognizes true sovereignty and gives his fealty rather to a drunken servant" (Brown 64). It is rather as if Moctezuma II had bowed down to Cortés's valet rather than to the great conquistador himself.

Near the end of the play Prospero, in the course of an elaborate and elaborately rhetorical boast of the powers of his "so potent art," powers of which we hear much but of which, except for the titular storm itself, we see little evidence in the play, where the arts practiced are primarily those of illusion, allows that the forces at his command are "Weak masters" in comparison with the demons summoned up by black magic, thus implicitly admitting his powers to be inferior to those of "the foul witch Sycorax." As is more explicitly acknowledged in the masque of the three goddesses acted out by sprites, Prospero's power in the play subsists largely in the performance of a spectacle of power, a pageant which produces the very power it purports to instantiate and represent. Like the English colonists, Prospero both conceals and overcomes his physical weakness (vis à vis the Indians or Caliban) by a staging of his metaphysical strength.

"Theatricality [in this most self-referentially theatrical of plays] is then not set over against power but is one of power's essential modes" (Greenblatt 33). I choose to read *The Tempest*'s almost brazen theatricalization of colonial power as a critique, well aware that it could also be read as that power's spectacle of self-congratulation at the effectiveness of the devices this performance lays bare.

WORKS CITED

Brown, Paul. "'This Thing of Darkness I Acknowledge Mine': *The Tempest* and the Discourse of Colonialism." *Political Shakespeare: New Essays in Cultural Materialism.* Ed. Jonathan Dollimore and Alan Sinfield. Ithaca: Cornell University Press, 1985.

Cartelli, Thomas. "Prospero in Africa: *The Tempest* as Colonialist Text and Pretext." *Shakespeare Reproduced: The Text in History and Ideology.* Ed. Jean E. Howard and Marian F. O'Connor. New York: Methuen, 1987.

Greenblatt, Stephen. "Invisible Bullets: Renaissance Authority and Its Subversion, *Henry IV* and *Henry V.*" *Political Shakespeare: New Essays in Cultural Materialism.* Ed. Jonathan Dollimore and Alan Sinfield. Ithaca: Cornell University Press, 1985.

Saving the Appearances

Adorno writes in *Aesthetic Theory* of art as apparition. I would like to rescue that fleeting, fragile, but tough-minded apparition from those who wish to dissipate it into the fog of an ideological mystification or the smoke of an unprofitable write-off.

1

There is a received wisdom among that small but vocal minority sometimes known as the cultural left (as distinct from any political left, which is more or less nonexistent in contemporary America) that equates bourgeois high culture with capitalism and its oppressions, though Peter Bürger notes that "whereas art forms owe their birth to a specific social context, they are not tied to the context of their origin or to a social situation that is analogous to it, for the truth is that they can take on different functions in varying social contexts" (69).

Both the current socio-political right and the current intellectual left reduce all values to those of socio-economic and political performativity, what Horkheimer and Adorno call instrumental reason. As Jean-François Lyotard writes, "Artistic and literary research is doubly threatened, once by the 'cultural policy' and once by the art and book market" (76). The "cultural policy" is today much more effectively that of the radical right than that of Lyotard's Stalinist specter, though both aim for what Herbert Marcuse described as affirmative culture. Andreas Huyssen notes that "the neo-conservative lament about the politicization of culture . . . is only ironic in this context since they themselves have a thoroughly political notion of culture" (206).

For the socio-political right, agents of capital whatever ideologies of "traditional values" they may flaunt, all human activities can be reduced to the pursuit or obstruction of profit. For the intellectual left, all can be reduced to the maintenance or subversion of bourgeois ideology. For seemingly wholly opposed ends, both sides participate in and perpetuate advanced capital's tyranny of the social, which like vulgar Marxism reduces all questions to those of economics. (Given that so many American leftists ignore economics altogether in favor of so-called cultural critique and cultural activism, perhaps such Marxism isn't so vulgar after all. Talking about money is always vulgar, isn't it?)

The attack on "bourgeois culture" as a purely negative goal seems much more important than the struggle toward a just and unalienated society to the radical academics whose social guilt leads them, without confronting their privileged positions within an educational system that functions largely as a vehicle of social exclusions, to call their pangs of conscience leftist or even Marxist. Denis Donoghue notes that the Western intelligentsia "show no sign of giving up bourgeois comfort but resent the society that provides it." (Parenthetically, the concepts of cultural pluralism and cultural activism function largely to displace desires for equality and democracy from the social to the aesthetic realm: a bracketing not everyone can afford.) They forget Lyotard's caveat that modernity consists in both the discovery of the lack of reality of reality *and* the invention of other realities (77). There must be a creative as well as a critical dimension. Such invention is one function of art, insofar as a function is demanded of it.

In his discussion of the absence of a "classical" avant-garde (an interestingly paradoxical notion, like the tradition of the new) in the United States, Huyssen implicitly recognizes that bourgeois culture has never played a central legitimating role for U.S. capitalism, for which it has been at worst irrelevant and at best another commodity. As Andrew Joron points out, "Any 'legitimation function' would be superfluous: the American machine, with its proudly exposed components of Accumulation and Repression, has no need for such a carapace" (4).

Having no classical institution of art, the U.S. could not develop or receive an equally classical negation of that institution. "Such an iconoclastic attack on cultural institutions . . . only made sense in countries where 'high art' had an essential role to play in legitimizing bourgeois political and social domination. . . . The cultural politics of 20th-century avantgardism would have been meaningless (if not regressive) in the United States, where 'high art' was still struggling hard to gain wider legitimacy and to be taken seriously by the public" (167). Huyssen argues that in the U.S. "high art [did become] institutionalized in the burgeoning museum, concert, and paperback culture of the 1950s," but immediately undercuts this argument by acknowledging that in the U.S. modernism "entered the mainstream via mass reproduction and the culture industry" (193).

In Adorno's words, "Society today has no use for art and its responses to it are pathological. In this society, art survives as reified cultural heritage and as a source of pleasure for the box-office customer, but ceases to have relevance as an object" (22). He goes on to write that a genuine experience of a work of art is a release, however fleeting and contingent, from the shackles of that society. "Happiness in the presence of works of art is a feeling of having made an abrupt escape" (22).

2

The historical avant-garde's attempted sublation of art into the praxis of life eulogized by Peter Bürger in *Theory of the Avant-Garde* has been fulfilled in the commodity aesthetics which moves beyond marketing objects to marketing experience itself. Capitalism has thus carried out what Marjorie Perloff calls the shift from a material to a situational aesthetic. (In Andrew Joron's description, "Here in America . . . 'culture' has been reduced to a simple play of intensities, to the simultaneously brutal and sentimental pulsions of mass media" [4].) Unlike Perloff, who in his terms might be said to be interested not in the new but merely in the novel, Bürger recognizes that such a sublation might not be wholly salutary. Rather than lifting up the quotidian, it has leveled the aesthetic: "the culture industry has brought about the false elimination of the distance between art and life, and this also allows one to recognize the contradictoriness of the avant-gardiste undertaking" (Bürger 50).

Perloff writes that "the aesthete's longing to protect art from the encroachments of industry . . . has dogged the artistic production of our century from the time of the Eiffel Tower to our own. It is the distinction of the *avant guerre* to have created the first artistic movement that tried to solve this problem, to break down the barriers between 'high' and 'low,' between, so to speak, the Ivory and the Eiffel towers" (201). In this regard, Perloff agrees with Bürger: both believe (Bürger in a much more self-critical fashion) that such a self-transcendence or self-negating of art as institution can be conducted by formal means, from within the institution of art. Contrarily, Martin Jay notes Habermas's caveat that "the utopian dedifferentiation of art *by itself* is insufficient to undo the pathologies of modernization." Indeed, by itself that dedifferentiation turns exactly into its dystopian opposite.

This is the much-noted aporia of the avant-garde: the historical avant-garde seeks to break down the walls between the institution of art and the praxis of life, but the praxis of life remains one of capitalist instrumentality. Thus, to collapse art into that praxis is to abdicate to capitalist social relations, and to close that space of critical and utopian thought which is the ground from which all such sorties set forth: "the (relative) freedom of art visá-vis the praxis of life is at the same time the condition that must be fulfilled if there is to be a critical cognition of reality. An art no longer distinct from the praxis of life but wholly absorbed in it will lose the capacity to criticize, along with its distance" (Bürger 50). To conflate, in critique or otherwise, capitalism and the bourgeois institution of art (as if art were more bourgeois than other institutions, as if art has not always been both complicit with and a reproach to domination) is to cooperate in capital's colonization of one of the few areas of social life not wholly absorbed by capital, collapsing art into culture and culture into society. (The academic institution commodifies and bureaucratizes creative discourse as much as any gallery or museum does, showing as insatiable an appetite as any television network for the new and improved products—legally described as "intellectual property"—by means of which academic discourse sustains and reproduces itself.) In Bürger's words, "Given the experience of the false sublation of autonomy, one will need to ask whether a sublation of the autonomy status [of art] can be desirable at all, whether the distance between art and the praxis of life is not requisite for that free space within which alternatives to what exists become conceivable" (54).

3

Art embodies the other-than, Ernst Bloch's principle of hope: a surplus, a utopian element that never fails or disappoints precisely because it is not. As an evocation of this possibility, I cite Jameson's description of "the classical [German] aesthetic, which projects . . . a Utopian realm of beauty and culture beyond the fallen empirical world of money and business activity, thereby winning a powerful critical and negative value through its capacity to condemn, by its very own existence, the totality of what is, at the same time forfeiting all [capacity for] social or political intervention in what is, by virtue of its constitutive disjunction or autonomy from society and history." However, I reject Jameson's valorization of negation, his reduction of the utopian potential of art to critique and refusal. Huyssen realizes that "out of negation alone, neither a new art nor a new society can be developed" (154). The affirmation of the contrary may operate as a mode of resistance to what Adorno and Horkheimer call the "commendation of the depressing everyday world" (cited in Huyssen 139), but as Huyssen points out, "the very notion of resistance [as set in opposition to affirmation] may be problematic. . . . There are affirmative forms of resistance and resisting forms of affirmation" (221). It is too often forgotten that Adorno's relentless negativity was in the service of a positive hope, the dream of an unalienated society. "Art is the promise of happiness, a promise that is constantly being broken" (Adorno 196).

The aesthetic, precisely because of its obsolescence, has become a category of possibilities other than (and not simply opposed to) those offered by commodity culture. But I don't wish to valorize art in purely ideological terms, as Bürger does. By such criteria the "oppositional" poem and the "oppositional" speech are indistinguishable, and the demand for an engaged literature becomes a capitulation to the ontological tyranny of things-as-they-are. As Adorno argues, "In art, direct protest is reactionary. Even critical art has to surrender itself to that which it opposes" (31). (This is not a prohibition on subject matter, as evidenced by Adorno's praise of Paul Celan.) Bürger's longing for a "political art" (by which he means an art whose content espouses a particular political tendency: as his argument makes clear, all art, like all other social practices, is inherently political), if fulfilled, can only transform an enabling uselessness into a despairing futility. As Abigail Solomon-Godeau writes of one of Bürger's examples, "John Heartfield's covers for *AIZ* (*Arbeiter Illustriete Zeitung*) had no discernible effect on the rise of fascism, although he was able to draw upon two important historic conditions unavailable to contemporary artists (a mass audience and a definable left culture)" (Ross 206).

Huyssen writes that "even under the conditions set by the capitalist culture industry and its distribution apparatus, art ultimately can open up emancipatory avenues only because it is granted autonomy and practical uselessness" (152). I would further assert that art can open up such avenues only by *means* of its uselessness, its abandonment of and by means-ends rationality. Art embodies and enacts a refusal of performativity by an alterity irreducible to the sum of its determinations.

Art preserves the possibility of liberation because its uselessness marks out a space not colonized by or valued by capital. Its "obsolescence" is also its resistance to being easily consumable; its loss of "relevance" is also a freedom to keep alive certain human possibilities. In Jameson's words, "the profound vocation of the work of art in a commodity society [is] *not* to be a commodity, *not* to be consumed" (395). Art offers an image of what Kant called the kingdom of ends, that other realm of freedom in which things and people exist for and in themselves and not as the means to something else. As Adorno asserts, "The utopia anticipated by artistic form is the idea that things at long last ought to come into their own" (195).

4

Contrary to the assertions of those whose socially-inflicted sufferings are merely spiritual, art is not a mode of social oppression. As a reservoir of values which society honors only in the breach, it functions exactly contrarily. "By their presence art works signal the possibility of the non-existent; their reality testifies to the feasibility of the unreal, the possible" (Adorno 192). For me growing up in the Bronx ghettoes, art pointed toward freedom; nor were "beauty" and "truth" dirty words. I have been oppressed by many things in my life, but not by art, which enacts potential rather than closure.

Art, like all human activities, occurs within social frameworks and contexts. This should be taken for granted. But this is not what distinguishes art from other social practices and institutions. Art is an institution and a social practice, but it is not *only* an institution and social practice. "Art is never coterminous with ideology" (Adorno 195). Elements of art escape social determination, and it is this excess which defines it as art. One cannot and should not erase an artwork's social context, but one can't and shouldn't replace the artwork with that context. If art is either condemned as ideology or valued only as oppositionality, then it vanishes as art. As Adorno reminds us, "There is nothing in art that does not derive from the world; and yet all that thus enters art is transformed" (201).

WORKS CITED

Adorno, Theodor. *Aesthetic Theory.* Trans. Christian Lenhardt. New York: Routledge and Kegan Paul, 1984.

Bürger, Peter. *Theory of the Avant-Garde.* Trans. Michael Shaw. Minneapolis: University of Minnesota Press, 1984.

Huyssen, Andreas. *After the Great Divide: Modernism, Mass Culture, Postmodernism.* Bloomington: Indiana University Press, 1986.

Jameson, Fredric. *Marxism and Form: Twentieth-Century Dialectical Theories of Literature.* Princeton: Princeton University Press, 1971.

Joron, Andrew. *The Cry at Zero: Selected Prose.* Denver: Counterpath Press, 2007.

Lyotard, Jean-François. *The Postmodern Condition: A Report on Knowledge.* Trans. Geoff Bennington and Brian Massumi. Minneapolis: University of Minnesota Pres, 1984.
Perloff, Marjorie. *The Futurist Moment: Avant-Garde, Avant-Guerre and the Language of Rupture.* Chicago: University of Chicago Press, 1986.
Ross, Andrew, ed. *Universal Abandon? The Politics of Postmodernism.* Minneapolis: University of Minnesota Press, 1988.

What Is Progressive Art?

The concepts of aesthetically progressive or reactionary art, of avant-garde or rearguard art, depend upon a teleological idea of history that derives from Hegel and has been most fully developed in relation to the arts by the critic and theorist Clement Greenberg and by the philosopher and critic Arthur C. Danto, who writes, in very Hegelian terms, that "it is possible to read twentieth-century art as the collective quest for the essence and nature of art" ("Approaching the End of Art," *State of the Art,* 204). I would like to offer a brief sketch of the history of this teleological notion of the history of art, in order to better illuminate what such terms as "progressive" or "avant-garde" art might mean for us today, especially given that, as Adorno points out, "the concept of progress is less directly applicable to art than it is to technical forces of production" (296). This is in no way a comprehensive survey, nor do I necessarily endorse the positions laid out here. I present them for consideration, as an historical perspective is often missing in discussions of the avant-garde. This discussion also raises the point made by Dana Arnold "that setting up the idea of artistic progress . . . implies that there is an end" to the history of art, an implication whose ramifications and consequences are worth considering.

1

In Hegel's theory of history, outlined in his *Introduction to the Theory of History,* first published in 1832, the course of history is the progress of Spirit (*Geist*) coming to consciousness of itself as Spirit, of consciousness coming to awareness of itself as consciousness. History is the self-realization of Spirit. Freedom is

Spirit's essence, and its goal is the complete realization of freedom, which Hegel defines as full self-consciousness: Spirit's unique capacity both to know and to be what it knows, to be simultaneously the object and the subject of knowledge. Every civilization represents Spirit's partial self-knowledge, and each civilization is superseded as Spirit moves on to a fuller self-realization. Though I will be using the term "Spirit" throughout this piece, in keeping with the standard translations, "Geist" can also be rendered as Mind, or even Consciousness.

In his *Philosophy of Fine Art* (published posthumously from lecture notes in 1835), Hegel works out this historical theory in terms of the arts. The history of art is the history of Spirit's search for material embodiment, seeking out forms that can physically manifest its inner tensions and resolutions. As Danto writes, "The story of art is the story of art's role in the grand history [one might call it, after Lyotard, the grand narrative] of the spirit."

In symbolic art, Spirit is only half-expressed, attempting to assert itself against its antithesis, matter, and finding expression in architectural forms like the Egyptian pyramids. At this stage, Spirit has not found a proper or adequate relationship to matter, is still unable to fully shape what Hegel calls "the purely material substance of nature." Thus, the relationship between object and meaning, matter and Spirit, is abstract and arbitrary. Spirit overflows and cannot be contained within its material embodiment.

In classical art, in Charles Altieri's summation, "the emphasis shifts to celebrating the integration of spirit with sensuous matter," the consecration of the sensuous, which we see in the idealized yet meticulously realistic figures of classical Greek sculpture, in which the body is raised up to the level of the sacred while still remaining wholly body. In classical art we find the perfect balance between idea and embodiment, content and form, Spirit and matter: as Hegel writes, "It is, in fact, the free and adequate embodiment of the idea in the shape which . . . is uniquely appropriate to the idea itself."

Finally, in romantic art, art becomes its own medium, the expression of Spirit in art itself, not merely in the objects represented in art. Just as symbolic art is exemplified by architecture and classical art by sculpture, romantic art is exemplified by painting, music, and poetry, in ascending order of freedom, idealization, and self-realization. Poetry is the highest art form, for its sensuousness is created by the mind, not by its materials. "In this way romantic art must be regarded as art transcending itself . . . in the form of itself."

In symbolic art, Spirit both overflows and is overwhelmed by matter. In classical art, Spirit finds its perfect embodiment in matter. In romantic art, Spirit triumphs over and withdraws from matter, moving from the external to the inner world. (Thus symbolic art and romantic art mirror one another: in each case there is a disproportion between Spirit and matter.) In Hegel's system, at this point art is superseded by philosophy, in which Spirit achieves its full and final articulation as Idea. So for Hegel, the history of art ends in the nineteenth century—not coincidentally, with the advent of his own philosophy. "According to Hegel, art was once the adequate mode of expression for spirit but has since ceased to be so" (Adorno 297). But the end of the history of art is not the end of art. In Hegel's words, "One may well hope that art will continue to advance and perfect itself, but its form has ceased to be the highest need of the spirit."

Hegel writes that "poetry is . . . the universal art of the mind, which has become essentially free, and which is not fettered in its realization to an externally sensuous material, but which is creatively active in the space and time belonging to the inner world of ideas and emotion. Yet it is precisely in this its highest phase, that art terminates, by transcending itself: it is just here that it deserts the medium of harmonious presentation of mind in sensuous shape and passes from the poetry of imaginative idea into the prose of thought." That is to say, as Spirit abandons the external world for the inner world, it also abandons the realm of sensuous embodiment, which art represents, for the realm of abstract thought, represented by philosophy.

Given the current debates regarding avant-garde, post-avant, or progressive poetry, it's interesting to note that for Hegel poetry is the most progressive of the arts. Indeed it's the end of art, both its culmination and its conclusion. Architecture is less ideal than sculpture, which is less ideal than painting, which is less ideal than music (which doesn't represent objects but sheer temporal order), which is less ideal than poetry, which eschews physical sensuousness for mental, virtual sensuousness. Thus poetry, as Aristotle wrote, is the most philosophical of the arts. Since philosophy, dealing as it does with pure concept, is in turn more ideal than poetry, it then succeeds and supersedes poetry. This list represents both temporal succession and synchronic distinction: the movement of Spirit is continually from embodiment to articulation.

2

For Clement Greenberg, the modern history of visual art is constituted by each medium's search for what is intrinsic and essential to it and each medium's discarding of all that is extrinsic and inessential, in particular whatever is shared by other media. "It seems to be a law of modernism—thus one that applies to almost all art that remains truly alive in our time—that the conventions not essential to the viability of a medium be discarded as soon as they are recognized. . . . And it is understood, I hope, that conventions are overhauled, not for revolutionary effect, but in order to maintain the irreplaceability and renew the vitality of art in the face of a society bent in principle on rationalizing everything. It is understood, too, that the devolution of tradition cannot take place except in the presence of tradition" ("'American-Type' Painting," *Art and Culture,* 208–9).

Interestingly, Greenberg sees the history of literature, in this sense, as having ended before that of painting: "This process of self-purification appears to have come to a halt in literature simply because the latter has fewer conventions to eliminate before arriving at those essential to it" ("'American-Type' Painting," 208). The model of the reduction to the essential is highly problematic when applied to literature. Literature's medium is language, which is not a thing but a relation, poised between materiality (sheer sound, sheer marks on the page) and immateriality (sheer concept). It is only in the conjunction between these two states that language exists as language. Thus, there is no essence down to which literature can be honed: it simply disappears.

The history of modern art is also the story of the shedding

of what is conventionally called subject matter, the elimination of representation: "Content is to be dissolved so completely into form that the work of art or literature cannot be reduced in whole or in part to anything not itself" ("Avant-Garde and Kitsch," 6). Thus narrative, along with all other literary effects, is discarded.

The history of modern painting is the story of the abandonment of sculptural effects (just as modern sculpture abandons pictorial effects) and of the illusion of three-dimensional space. The painting reduces itself to the flat picture plane. For Greenberg this reduction is also an expansion: "The picture plane as a whole imitates visual experience as a whole; rather, the picture plane as a total object represents space as a total object" ("On the Role of Nature in Modernist Painting," *Art and Culture,* 173). This process culminates in abstract expressionism and color field painting, in which the paint literally sinks into and becomes one with the surface of the canvas. As Kirk Varnedoe explains in his *Pictures of Nothing,* "In the eyes of Greenberg, [Michael] Fried, and [William] Rubin, modern art had an innate tendency to pull away from any literary reference to things outside itself and to refer only to the essential properties of painting per se: flatness, line, and color. By staining their paint directly into raw canvas, [Kenneth] Goldsmith, [Morris] Louis, and [Helen] Frankenthaler had eliminated any residual sense of space, becoming even more abstract than [Jackson] Pollock" (98–99). After these developments come pop art, minimalism, and conceptual art, which for Greenberg are simply not part of the history of art at all.

Greenberg's most succinct and comprehensive summation of this view of the history of modern art is to be found in his 1960 essay "Modernist Painting," in which he writes that "what had to be exhibited was not only that which was unique and irreducible in art in general, but also that which was unique and irreducible in each particular art. Each art had to determine, through its own operations and works, the effects exclusive to itself" (*Collected Essays,* 86).

Though Greenberg never mentions Hegel, this is a clearly Hegelian notion: the history of art is the history of art coming to consciousness of its essence as art, and of each medium coming to consciousness of its essence as a medium. It is the history of art's progressive self-consciousness and self-awareness. As Varnedoe points out, "Greenberg's theory of form and formal development is Hegelian and leads toward increasing perfection of realization" (153).

3

The philosopher and art critic Arthur C. Danto has further developed this Hegelian model. Whereas for Greenberg the history of modern art is the story of each medium discovering and reducing itself to its essence, for Danto that history is the story of the pursuit of the smallest distinction between art and life, the zero degree of difference. For Danto, this zero degree was reached with Andy Warhol's *Brillo Box,* which posed the question of why one object is art when objects identical to it are not.

I'm not sure why Duchamp's readymades, most famously his 1917 *Fountain,* didn't pose exactly this same question, or how, as an actual urinal exhibited in an art gallery, it failed to embody the zero degree of difference between art and non-art. Danto acknowledges this in *The Abuse of Beauty,* in which he writes that "there is a metaphysical question in distinguishing between *Fountain* and the urinal it consisted of, not altogether different from distinguishing between a person and his or her body" (12). In *Beyond the Brillo Box,* Danto writes that "Dada believed itself a form of artistic freedom but in fact was merely a style," but doesn't explain what he means. Perhaps the difference is that Duchamp took an actual utilitarian object from the quotidian world and placed it within the frame of art, thus both asking us to look at this mundane object as art and asking us to question what art is and what can count as art. Warhol, on the other hand, produced an aesthetic object that is indistinguishable from the utilitarian object in the quotidian world: he made something that one might call a perfect simulacrum. Duchamp's urinal really was the object; Warhol's *Brillo Box* was an artwork identical to the object.

However, Danto notes in *The Abuse of Beauty* that Warhol's *Brillo Box* was in fact not identical to the object, but only a copy, though he doesn't seem to recognize the ways in which this fact undermines his argument. Warhol's *Brillo Box* was made of painted plywood, whereas industrially produced Brillo boxes are made of printed corrugated cardboard. Danto writes that Warhol's *Brillo Box* "looked enough like the commercial cartons in which Brillo pads were packed that a photograph of one would look entirely like a photograph of the other" (23–24). But this does not mean that the objects themselves looked entirely like one another, only that, hypothetically, representations of them would (and not even that they actually did or do)—a very different thing. I have not seen Warhol's Brillo boxes in person, but I doubt that a close visual inspection would find them identical to commercial Brillo boxes. And sight is not the only sense. The texture, the smell, and even the sound of the boxes when tapped or thumped would be different. So in fact, they are not identical, not indiscernible, at all.

Danto shows himself to be a true Hegelian when he asserts that at this point, the occasion of Andy Warhol's *Brillo Box* exhibit of 1964, "the history of art attained that point where it had to turn into its own philosophy. It had gone, as art, as far as it could go. In turning into philosophy, art had come to an end. From now on progress could only be enacted on a level of abstract self-consciousness of the kind which philosophy alone must consist in. . . . Painting does not stop when it ends like this. But it enters what I like to term its post-historical period" ("Approaching the End of Art," 216).

In *Aesthetic Theory*, Theodor Adorno, writing also from an explicitly Hegelian position, makes an argument that proleptically rebukes Danto's: "A consistently rational and elaborated work, because of its absolute autonomy, would tend to level the distinction between art and empirical being, assimilating itself to commodities without directly imitating them. It would be indistinguishable from perfectly functional creations except in one respect: it would have no purpose, and that would speak against it" (310). Contrary to Danto's assertion, the art object indistinguishable from the empirical object would be inferior to the utilitarian object, because it would have no function, while simultaneously it would have lost or given up art's purposive purposelessness. That would be the end of art in a wholly negative sense. The artwork would simply become a failed, because useless, commodity.

For Danto, the history of art is over, which is a kind of liberation: one is no longer a prisoner of progress as either an artist or a spectator. The end of art history means, among others, that it is now possible to practice and appreciate a wide and eclectic range of art practices, that all the artistic modes, genres, and techniques of the past are now fully available to the contemporary artist, since he or she need no longer be ruled by concern over his or her contribution to or place within the forward march of artistic history. It means that the artist is free, that everything and anything can be admitted into the realm of art. In Danto's summation,

> this means returning art to the serving of largely human [and/or individual] ends. . . . It is no mean thing for art that it should now be an enhancement of human life. And it was in its capacity as such an enhancement that Hegel supposed that art would go on even after it had come to an end. It is only that he did not suppose happiness to be the highest vocation to which a spiritual existence is summoned. For him, the highest vocation is self-knowledge, and this he felt was to be achieved by philosophy. Art went as far as it can in this direction, toward philosophy, in the present century. This is what he would have meant by saying [that] art reaches its end. The comparison with philosophy is not intended as invidious. Philosophy too comes to an end, but unlike art it really must stop when it reaches its end, for there is nothing for it to do when it has fulfilled its task. ("Approaching the End of Art," 217–18)

For Wittgenstein, contrarily, philosophy's task after the end of philosophy (which of course ends with him) is to enrich, clarify, and enlighten human life, the same task that Hegel and Danto assign to art after its demise.

4

Peter Bürger, in his *Theory of the Avant-Garde,* offers a politically inflected version of a similar idea, one which explicitly conjoins the artistic avant-garde and the political avant-garde. For Bürger, the end of art is both its culmination and its dissolution as an independent entity. Bürger makes a distinction between Modernism, which he sees as a purely aesthetic phenomenon engaged with the formal evolution of the medium, and is exemplified by Cubism, and the avant-garde, which is a larger-scaled phenomenon aimed at the transformation of human existence. In Bürger's formulation, the historical avant-garde, which contra Danto is exemplified for him by Dada, and also by Russian Constructivism (different as these two movements were in their methods and intentions), aims at the sublation of the institution of art into the praxis of life, the merging of art and life. For Bürger, the avant-garde is an historical phenomenon. It failed in its aims, or its aims were achieved only in distorted, parodic form: "The culture industry has brought about the false elimination of the distance between art and life, and this also allows one to recognize the contradictoriness of the avant-gardiste undertaking" (50). Bürger also realizes that, since the praxis of life in our society remains one of capitalist instrumentality, to collapse art into that praxis is to surrender to capitalist social relations, and to close that space of critical and utopian possibility which art offers:

> The (relative) freedom of art vis-á-vis the praxis of life is at the same time the condition that must be fulfilled if there is to be a critical cognition of reality. An art no longer distinct from the praxis of life but wholly absorbed in it will lose the capacity to criticize [or to propose other possibilities], along with its distance. . . . Given the experience of the false sublation of autonomy, one will need to ask whether a sublation of the autonomy status [of art] can be desirable at all, whether the distance between art and the praxis of life is not requisite for that free space within which alternatives to what exists become conceivable. (50, 54)

Adorno anticipated this realization when he wrote that "to call for the abolition of art in a society that is moving from partial to total barbarism is to invite co-optation by that society" (356).

5

The phrase "avant-garde," first attested in French in 1910, originally derives from the context of war. With regard to the arts, and to poetry in particular, what war are we fighting, and against whom or what? On what battlefront or toward what target are we advancing? Ironically, in this context, to be "post-avant" is to be taking up the rear, to be, in fact, in the rearguard. But then, the vanguard, the "avant-garde," was often made up of troops considered expendable, cannon fodder on whom the enemy could expend their artillery to make the way easier for the troops who followed them.

It should be kept in mind that all motion is forward motion, that is, progress, because time moves only in one direction, forward. We are always progressing from one state to another, which says nothing about the quality or value of either our motion or the states we are leaving behind or moving toward. Progress, perhaps, but progress toward what? Hegel and Greenberg, at least, had clear ideas of what history and artistic history were moving toward. But Wallace Stevens reminds us that "one cannot spend one's time in being modern when there are so many more important things to be." One also cannot help but be modern, which makes worrying about how modern one is a bit beside the point.

I'd like to thank my partner, Robert Philen, for his insights that much improved and enriched this piece.

WORKS CITED

Adorno, Theodor. *Aesthetic Theory.* Trans. Christian Lenhardt. New York: Routledge and Kegan Paul, 1984.

Bürger, Peter. *Theory of the Avant-Garde.* Trans. Michael Shaw. Minneapolis: University of Minnesota Press, 1984.

Danto, Arthur C. *The Abuse of Beauty: Aesthetics and the Concept of Art.* Chicago: Open Court Publishing Company, 2003.

Danto, Arthur C. *Beyond the Brillo Box: The Visual Arts in Post-Historical Perspective.* New York: Farrar Straus Giroux, 1992.

Danto, Arthur C. *The State of the Art.* New York: Prentice Hall, 1987.

Frascina, Francis, and Charles Harrison, eds. *Modern Art and Modernism: A Critical Anthology*. Scranton, PA: HarperCollins, 1983.

Greenberg, Clement. *Art and Culture: Critical Essays*. Boston: Beacon Press, 1961.

Greenberg, Clement. *The Collected Essays and Criticism, Volume 4: Modernism with a Vengeance, 1957–1969*, ed. John O'Brien. Chicago: University of Chicago Press, 1993.

Varnedoe, Kirk. *Pictures of Nothing: Abstract Art since Pollock*. Princeton: Princeton University Press, 2006.

Artistic Production

Marx, Labor, and the Artist

Since so many artists and writers are, are considered to be, or consider themselves to be some variety of Marxist (sometimes quasi-Marxist, pseudo-Marxist, faux-Marxist, or Marxist manqué), I thought that it might be interesting to lay out Marx's views on what Walter Benjamin called the artist as producer: the artist as cultural worker in the same way that someone laboring in a factory is an industrial worker. I don't address Marx's views on the content of literature or art, but rather focus on the Marxist structural analysis of the artist's place in the relations of production, and the ideological penumbra which surrounds that position. In Marx's words, "The mode of production of material life conditions the social, political and intellectual life process in general. It is not the consciousness of men that determines their being, but, on the contrary, their social being that determines their consciousness" (*Contribution to the Critique of Political Economy*).

It should also go without saying that I don't agree with all that's laid out here. As I have written on many occasions, while social circumstances condition the production of art, they don't determine its forms, its meaning, or its value, though those circumstances do inform these things. Art can and must exceed social circumstance and social determination, as Marx and Engels recognized (in wholly ideological terms) in their discussion of *La Comédie Humaine:* the work's accuracy and truth content, exposing the corruption of nineteenth-century French bourgeois society, made it socially progressive despite Balzac's reactionary, monarchist views. Whatever my reservations, I often find Marxist structural analysis both interesting and useful. I present it here for the sake of historical and intellectual perspective. I use the masculine pronoun throughout because Marx does.

Marx discusses the product of labor as the objectification of labor, which under the best of circumstances is the realization of the potentiality of the laborer and his productive capacities. As he puts it, human beings produce themselves through labor. In capitalist society, the worker is alienated from both the process and the product of his labor, working under conditions and at tasks not of his own choosing to create a product not of his own choosing which he does not own and which will not benefit him: the commodity. (Marx distinguishes between production to fulfill the needs of the producer and production in order to acquire the means to fulfill those needs.) Thus the realization of labor which should function as the fulfillment of his productive capacities functions for the worker as a loss of reality, for those capacities have been stolen from him. The object he produces, labor's product, is "something alien . . . a power independent of the producer. The product of labor is labor which has been congealed in an object, which has become material: it is the *objectification* of labor. Labor's realization is its objectification" (*Economic and Philosophic Manuscripts of 1844*). All human capacities seek a fulfillment in the material world, but because the worker exercises his capacities as someone else ("I" is an other not just for Rimbaud), as the agent of the owner of the means of production, whose interests not only diverge from but contradict his own, this fulfillment is distorted. The object which the worker produces under these conditions, the commodity, is therefore the sign or, as Marx writes, the summary of the alienation of his labor activities.

Artistic production is a particular case of production in general. In modern Western society, at least since the Romantic period, the artist has been imagined as the prototype and ideal of the unalienated worker: he objectifies (that is, expresses) his productive capacities (that is, his "self," his imagination or genius) directly and without constraint. If workers put their lives into the objects they produce, then their lives no longer belong to them but to those objects, because they neither own nor choose to produce those objects. But for the artist, who chooses both the means and the result of his own production, his art is a fulfillment of his productive capacities, because both the impulse and the product of his labor are his own. Man exists as a productive being: thus, the artist's life is his own. As Marx writes in *The German Ideology*, "As individuals express their life, so they are. What they are, therefore, coincides with their production, both with *what* they produce and with *how* they produce. The nature of individuals thus depends on the material conditions determining their production."

The ideology of genius expresses this idea of the artist's free and autonomous production. The artist is exempt from the pressures of productive life. His labor activity derives from some transcendent yet uniquely individual source, wholly personal in origin yet universal in the significance of its outcome, the artwork which is both the product of the artist's labor as cultural worker and the tangible manifestation of his spiritual freedom (that is, of his free command over his own productive capacities). Whereas for the ordinary worker his labor is external to himself, the artist's labor is uniquely his own. The worker denies himself in his labor; the artist affirms himself in his. The artist's labor is not just the means to satisfy a need, but is itself the satisfaction of a need.

But because capitalist society cannot conceive of genuinely unforced labor, the artist's labor has been conceived of as being at the service of a "genius" external and superior to him, whose necessity is his freedom. (We find this conception in Hegel, who calls this transcendent force finding immanent form *Geist*, Spirit.) To slightly twist a formulation of Marx's, just as in religion "the spontaneous activity of the human imagination . . . operates independently of the individual—that is, operates on him as an alien, divine, or diabolical activity—in the same way the [artist's] activity is not his spontaneous activity. It belongs to another [not, in this case, the capitalist, but the Muse, the *daimon*, the inspiration upon which he depends]; it is the loss of self" (*Economic and Philosophic Manuscripts of 1844*). In the ideology of genius, the artist loses himself in his possession by his own genius, which is both intrinsic to him and alien to him. The artist's uniqueness depends on a mystified refusal of his generality, as well as on a willed self-alienation intended to stave off the imposed alienation of capitalist society. "The illusory quality art has (in so far as it pretends to be an in-itself) points to the fact that, despite the impression of total subjective mediation, art partakes of the universal blindness and reification surrounding it. In Marxist terms, art cannot help but reflect a relationship of living labor as though it were congealed into an object. The consistency of art works is the aspect that enables them to share in the truth, but it also implicates them in falsehood" (Adorno 242). Art is thus a special case of the isolation and atomization of the individual in capitalist society.

Paradoxically, the idea of the free artist was dependent upon the development of the free market: that is, of an economy based on money exchange rather than on what Marx rather idealistically refers to as "natural" relations of production and exchange, in which there is a direct relation between production and consumption (that is, needs). Under feudalism, the artist was explicitly the agent and objectifier of a social vision: his relation to the ideology of which he was both servant and creator, as enacted in his relation to a patron either aristocratic or clerical (and often both), was both direct and unforced. His place in the relations of production and its accompanying social arrangements was represented without mediation or mystification.

The modern idea of the artist depends on the shift in this relation from one to an individual patron to one with the market in general, in which the artwork is in competition not only with other artworks but with other forms of cultural production. The idea of genius can thus be read as a technique of advertising and publicity, a means by which a particular artist and those who invest in his work (the employers who derive surplus value from his labor in the form of profit as the artwork "appreciates" in value) differentiate this product both generally (as "art") and specifically (from other artworks) from other products on the cultural market. It also serves as a replacement guarantor of value for his activities as they become more marginal to society's ideological self-constitution. As Marx wrote, "The exclusive concentration of artistic talent in certain individuals and its consequent suppression in the broad masses of the people is an effect of the capitalist division of labor" (quoted in Stevens, 206).

The artist thus maintains a precarious link to the activity and product of his labor by emphasizing and deepening (both as a form of promotion and as a mode of distinguishing his labor activity from that of the ordinary worker) his alienation both from society (given that in capitalist society one's place in the division of labor *is* one's social and thus one's individual definition) and from *general* human powers. Hence the definition of art as an activity and an object depends upon its clear demarcation from all other human activities, including all those others in which the artist, as a social being, inevitably participates. The artist expresses his true self only through the occlusion of himself as a social being.

WORKS CITED

Adorno, Theodor. *Aesthetic Theory.* Trans. Christian Lenhardt. New York: Routledge and Kegan Paul, 1984.

Marx, Karl. *A Contribution to the Critique of Political Economy.*

Marx, Karl. *Economic and Philosophic Manuscripts of 1844.*

Marx, Karl. *The German Ideology.*

Stevens, Bernard. "The Soviet Union." *European Music in the Twentieth Century.* Ed. Howard Hartog. New York: Frederick A. Praeger, 1957.

Some Issues in the Teaching of Creative Writing

The Institutional Context

Due to the heavily policed institutional borders between creative writing and criticism or literature, the interrelationship of the two is often obscured. Creative writers, seeing themselves as the keepers of the sacred flame of literature, engage in frequent polemics against the destructive encroachments of theory on creativity, while theorists largely ignore or at best disdain the unselfconscious effusions of authors who refuse to accept the news of their death.

This state of affairs has always troubled me, for I have never felt the chasm between my writing and my critical intellect (or that between my emotions and my thoughts on which it is based) that so many seem not only to take for granted but determined to enforce on others. Other literary works, both those with which I have felt affinities and those toward which I've felt great antipathy, have always been both inspirations for and challenges to my own work and the work I aspired to do. Indeed, I never would have considered the possibility of writing poetry without the impetus of reading deeply in it, wanting to comprehend, apprehend, and wield the power I found in it.

Complementarily, criticism and what is sweepingly and too vaguely called "theory" have been very useful in thinking through my own writing, and have helped me work through many an impasse in my poetry. This is what the best literary criticism does and should do: elucidate and illuminate literature for readers and for writers.

Most literary academics have no idea how to read a poem,

having imbibed the conviction that close reading or textual explication is reactionary or simply passé without ever having informed themselves about just what such reading might entail. While poetry writing programs have burgeoned, poetry has fallen by the wayside as an object of literary study in favor of the examination of novels as social documents. As Barbara K. Fischer has recently noted, "Despite sporadic resurgences, poetry has for several decades occupied a marginalized position in English departments, where fiction and popular culture have become the preferred objects of analysis. The New Criticism, with its heuristic approach to analyzing a poem's tropes and formal construction, left a generation of students with a distaste for the seemingly clinical task of 'explication'—the dreaded homework assignment. Meanwhile, New Critical aestheticism—its emphasis on the poem as a self-referential *objet d'art,* isolated from politics and the conditions of its making—was set up over and over again as a straw man for the arguments that comprised the revolutions in critical thinking of the 1970s through 1990s. As poststructuralists, New Historicists, and many others challenged the New Critical paradigm, they also demoted poetry as the privileged object of literary study."

Many literary scholars and theorists believe that writing cannot or should not be taught, that talent is some immeasurable intangible. Many creative writers, some of them teachers of creative writing, share this belief. Such academics share many students' sense that there is nothing to teach or be taught in a creative writing class, that writing literature, unlike, presumably, analyzing or theorizing it, requires no knowledge or training. Reified notions of innate genius which have been thoroughly deconstructed with regard to the literatures of the past are still too often unselfconsciously applied by writers and by critics to dismiss the possibility of training the writers of future literatures. Some people have a greater aptitude than others for musical composition or performance, for dance, for science or mathematics, yet no one asserts on that basis that these practices cannot be taught. Nor would many argue against the assertion that both those with more of an inclination and those with less of an inclination toward such pursuits can benefit from such education and training. But among both writers and critics, canards like "Keats never took a writing workshop" are freely tossed about, although the most cursory scan of literary history shows that developing writers and artists have always engaged in formal and informal processes of apprenticeship and training, of learning from and being guided by more experienced artists and writers. Perhaps it is the wider availability these days of such apprenticeships to *hoi polloi* to which critics of creative writing programs object. Historically, Keats is one of the few poets born in the working classes to have been able to take advantage of such apprenticeship and patronage.

The idea that writing cannot be taught is a more sophisticated version of the emptied-out pseudo-romanticism pervasive in our society: the assumption that everything one needs is inside one, that thought is the enemy of creativity and of feeling in general, that self-awareness is antithetical to art. As Ann Lauterbach has put it, "There's a familiar split in the notion of what a creative act is. That split, in our culture, involves an idea of creativity as being natural and expressive: a poet has no need to have thought about anything in order to make a poem; the enemy is the analytical. This is a long-standing divisive space, certainly within the academy but also in the culture at large" (Bernstein et al. 196). But self-awareness, the capacity to step back and analyze not just the world but oneself, is what defines us as human, and art is the material embodiment of that self-awareness, of the capacity to separate oneself from one's immediate existence and see it as if from the outside. In that regard, art and science, often conceived of as opposites, have a great deal in common: both are about not taking for granted things as they appear, neither the world nor oneself, about investigating and exploring the universe rather than simply existing in it, about delving through the surfaces of things to understand their true workings. Things are not always what or how they seem, and we are among those things.

In English departments there is little or no attention paid to contemporary literature, except for that literature which can be scrutinized (as distinct from being actually read) as a social symptom, minority and women's literature for the most part. (I must add, though, that I have never encountered the caricatured straw institution so prevalent in right-wing anti-academic screeds where Hopi chants are taught instead of Shakespeare.) In most creative writing programs, only contemporary literature is read, and there is a pervasive neglect of the literature of the past (especially of anything written before the twentieth century) among both students and faculty, who tend to consider it irrelevant or even (if they are a bit more intellectually hip) oppressive. Individual students may make efforts to educate themselves, but they are rarely given any context or structure in which to do so, or any incentive for their efforts.

Students in creative writing courses and programs too often expect their work to emerge from the vacuum of inspiration (a vacuum too easily filled with prepackaged formulations and received ideas, from popular music, television, and movies, among other sources); some of their teachers share this expectation. The intention of the writer is conflated with the intention of the poem, because no other context is provided or produced for the work: thus the role of the creative writing teacher is simply to facilitate the student in finding and perhaps refining his or her own voice. This voice is assumed by students and teachers alike to be pre-existent, needing at most to be shaped and developed. Each student brings an idiosyncratic and haphazard canon and set of assumptions to the class, basing his or her ideas of poetry on what he or she happens to have read or to have heard on the radio (for many students, popular music lyrics are their main model of poetry). Rarely have they read enough to have made informed choices among the possibilities of writing practice or to have questioned choices made solely on the basis of "what I like." I have heard creative writing instructors say that they specifically exclude outside reading from their classes in order to focus on student work, as if that work came forth with no connection to any other writing.

The unacknowledged assumptions underpinning both student reading and student writing (the reification of taste, the valorization of sincerity, the enshrinement of self-expression) block the development of each individual's writing, leaving students in cul-de-sacs inescapable precisely because they are invisible. Even students engaged in experimental modes tend not to have read anything outside those modes, any of the work that led up to or even negatively instigated that work. Moreover, they are frequently unwilling or unable to recognize what is still radical (in both senses of the word) or experimental about writers like Sir Thomas Wyatt or Christopher Marlowe, should they take the occasion to read them. Many young writers' conception of "the experimental" seems a concoction of received ideas about "Language" poetry (as if other kinds of poetry were made of something other than language) and an attenuated romantic notion of idiosyncratic individualism. Thus such writers are often also ignorant of and uninterested in the historical and intellectual underpinnings of those modes, seeing them only as matters of style. Anti-intellectualism and an indifference to literary history are rife among both mainstream and avant-garde writers.

Some Stumbling Blocks in the Creative Writing Classroom

Students come to creative writing courses with three major impediments to learning the art and craft of writing. First, they tend to assume that, because they speak English and are at least officially literate (though some lack basic mechanical writing skills), they know how to write poems. This is something one encounters to a much lesser degree in other artistic media: because people don't work with pigments or clay on a daily basis, they don't have quite the same conviction that they already know how to paint or how to sculpt. (Though it is true that painting or sculpting students often cultivate a premature sense of their own expertise, of what is or is not relevant for them to know how to do.) But because language is used and abused as a medium of exchange in everyday life, students (like people in general) find it very difficult to conceive of it as an *artistic* medium.

In literature courses, students usually (though not always) agree that the professor has not only read *Paradise Lost* or *King Lear,* but that she or he knows more about these texts than they do, though they often question the point of such knowledge. But students tend to enter creative writing classes unconvinced that there's a subject to be taught at all—the class is simply the forum for them to express what's already inside them, to do what they already know how to do. A common expression of this is the assertion that creative writing is too personal or subjective to judge, criticize, or grade. Some of the work one has to do in such a class is simply to persuade them that it's a class at all. A student once said to me, "You act like you know more than everyone else in the room." I explained that she would have had cause to complain if I *didn't* know more than they did (at least about the topic at hand).

There is nothing wrong with writing only for oneself, or for one's boyfriend or girlfriend, with writing as a purely private act, a hobby like collecting different mixes of one's favorite song. But when one takes a class in creative writing, one is implicitly bringing one's writing into a public forum, agreeing to its terms of judgment (however various), and placing one's work in the larger context of what has been and is being written. One is staking a claim, however contingent, to a place in literary culture, in writing as an artistic practice. That is, one is deciding *not* simply to write for oneself. Indeed, one of the most valuable things that students can learn from a creative writing course is to see their work from the outside, to see it as others see it—that is, as readers. If a student learns actually to *read* his or her own work (and hopefully that of her or his classmates, and that of the assigned writers), then I have at least in part succeeded.

This leads directly to the second impediment to student learning in creative writing courses: students find it very hard to separate themselves, their thoughts and feelings, or at best the subject of the poem, from the poem on the page, whether it's a poem they have written or a poem someone else has. Indeed, they are often literally unable to see what they have written, because what they meant to say fills their vision to the exclusion of anything else, very much including the particular words that they have put down on the page. To ask, "What does this line say on the literal level?" is too often to hear a long explanation of every thought in the student's head related to the line in question *except* those that might illuminate why these particular words occur in this particular order at this particular point in this particular poem. Frequently one receives a narrative of the incident that inspired the poem. These anecdotes can sometimes be more interestingly vivid and specific than the poem, to the extent that I will sometimes tell a student, "Write that down.

That's the poem." Students sometimes don't even know the definitions of the words that they use, and will frequently dismiss such knowledge as unimportant—since poetry means anything that you want it to mean.

Because students look at their own poems and see not the words they have written but the thoughts, emotions, and experiences the words point to, they tend to write poems as captions to pictures that aren't there, providing the meaning of something that isn't present. The meaning is presented without giving the reader the object or situation that would actually be doing the meaning. If they do include images and concrete particulars, they will often not trust those to convey the meaning or "message" without such commentary or explanation.

This also means that students look not only at their own poems but at those of their classmates and those they may be assigned to read purely in terms of what they mean or (assumedly) intend to mean: they like a poem because they like or identify with its subject matter, and dislike a poem because they don't. The poem is purely a vessel or vehicle of subject matter, any of whose surface complexities are mere impediments to grasping that matter. Any poem that doesn't have an immediately identifiable topic will often be dismissed as pretentious nonsense, except among those students who have decided that nonsense is the definition of poetry.

As any teacher of creative writing knows, students take criticism of their writing as criticism of themselves in a way that usually doesn't happen in literature courses. To tell a student that her poem about her son, for example, is sentimental can be taken as an attack on her maternal feelings. This also applies to getting students to provide substantive criticism of their peers' work, which often feels mean to them. About the only work that students feel free to criticize is that which the instructor has assigned, since in general the instructor's viewpoint counts for less than anyone else's in the room (after all, he or she is neither a potential date, a dorm-mate, nor a drinking buddy).

To provide students with feedback that is both honest and usable, couched in terms which they can understand, to encourage them to real effort without misleading them about the challenges such effort entails, to point out ways in which their productions are not yet aesthetic objects while not making them feel that they have failed at a task in which they have no hope of success, to point out potentials in their poems without misleading them into thinking that those potentials have already been realized, is a delicate balancing act. Constantly telling students that their work is wonderful does them a great educational disservice and makes it more difficult for them to become better writers. Too harshly judging their tentative steps into a realm many of them have never before explored makes them despairing and angry, and ensures that they will never hear anything you say.

This is a problem found at the graduate level as well, where students' personal investment in their work is mixed with a premature professionalization and a conviction that they are already Poets (very much with the capital P): insecurity and vulnerability commingle with arrogance and a sense of entitlement.

The third impediment to the teaching and learning of creative writing is that students are very resistant to reading. They want to write poems without having read poems, and frequently their only models for poems are pop song lyrics and greeting cards. Far from understanding that poetry comes out of poetry, or that they can learn from reading the poetry of others, they too often see reading as an impediment to their free self-expression. As a student once asked me, "Why are you making us read all this stuff and stifling our creativity?"

Obviously, students in all courses and all disciplines are often resistant to reading, resistant to working at all. Many students see attending classes and doing schoolwork as an imposition on their time. (One student rather disarmingly admitted during a class discussion of Shakespeare's sonnets that "I can understand this when I work at it, but I don't like having to work.") And students, like people in general, frequently value their own notions and opinions more than whatever some book might have to tell them. But creative writing students tend to dislike reading not just out of laziness or self-involvement, but out of a sense that it is actively antithetical to their own "creative process." It rarely occurs to them to ask who would want to read the writings of those who are themselves unwilling to read. Indeed, the idea of audience rarely occurs to them at all.

Many students attend college for no reason other than having been told that is what they should do after high school, and perhaps with the hope that they will make more money if they have a college degree. They tend to feel simultaneously resentful ("Here I am stuck in this stupid class") and entitled ("I'm not in high school anymore, now I'm an adult"). Students often see creative writing classes as the antithesis to their other classes, in which they are forced to absorb and regurgitate all kinds of information in which they have no personal interest or investment. In a creative writing class, they can be themselves, because anything goes in a poem. They also believe that poetry is too subjective to judge, because it's all opinion and personal preference.

To acknowledge that personal preference and opinion are always factors while still maintaining that specificity, particularity of image and language, precision, concision, and avoidance of cliché are aspects of all good poetry (as sometimes needs to be pointed out, vagueness is not a style) sometimes seems beyond them, especially since they are convinced and have often been taught that if they think something then it must be true. (One great problem in American education isn't what students don't know, but what they know that isn't true.) My partner has a bumper sticker on his office door that reads, "Don't believe everything you think." It's a caution that many might profitably take to heart.

We live in a culture which robs people of social, political, and economic agency, making them feel as if their experience counts for nothing, while simultaneously insisting that everyone's every passing notion and experience is of supreme importance because it happened to *them.* These two aspects are concomitant with one another, the second offering an imaginary (that is, an ideological) compensation for the first. Much of the boom both in creative writing programs and in slam poetry, performance poetry, stand-up poetry, and the like, has more to do with a cult of the public performance of personality (à la Oprah Winfrey and Jerry Springer), on the one hand, and with the scarcity of outlets for genuine feeling and expression in our society and an ever-increasing sense of the impotence and insignificance of the individual, on the other hand, than with an interest in poetry as an art form.

The turn to creative writing, and to versions of poetry in particular, is a way of saying "I matter" in a wholly ritualized and conventionalized format, and is wholly understandable (if somewhat misdirected) as such. But again, this has to do not with an interest in the art of poetry, but rather with a sense that poetry is a mode of personal expression unsullied by commerce or social constraints. (And poems are shorter and thus apparently easier to write than novels or even short stories, another aspect of their appeal in a society that seeks quick results but shuns effort.) So the recent rise in the popularity of poetry doesn't contradict poetry's marginality in our culture any more than does the use of the word "poetry" as an all-purpose honorific: Michael Jordan, as they say, was poetry in motion on the basketball court. I prefer to think that poetry is poetry and basketball is basketball. Indeed, it is one of the functions of art to help us see things as and for themselves.

Canonical poetry, or literary poetry, or Modernist poetry, or post-Modernist poetry, or any poetry grounded in a practice of language and of writing as such, rather than one of personal expressivity and/or identity confirmation, still isn't much read. Rather, it is disdained as one or another variety of stiff academicism, insular, "elitist," and oppressive, as opposed to the authentic expression of slam poetry, for example. In this model, "creativity" is just another commodity which anyone can procure, on credit if necessary.

A Few Solutions for the Creative Writing Classroom

Making reading, both of contemporary poetry and of the poetic tradition, central to the workshop process expands the realm of poetic possibilities for students by exposing them to work that can challenge their assumptions about what poetry is, can be, and should be. "Canonical" work, when actually *read,* can be as unsettling and exploratory as explicitly avant-garde work. Indeed, there is no such homogeneous literary past as the singular term "canon" suggests—the idea of a monolithic canon is a pedagogical fiction, throwing together works that if taken seriously often cancel one another out. Nor is there any such absolute divide between traditional and experimental: if actually *read,* T. S. Eliot's poems are as radical now as when they were first written. Such avowed opponents as John Hollander and Charles Bernstein, however antithetical their ideological positions, share the conviction that the matter of poems is words and their relations.

By emphasizing and making explicit the contextual and intertextual nature of all writing (did I invent the words I am using now? did I create this syntax or produce this grammar?), and by exposing students to the polymorphous and often contentious nature of literatures in the plural, the integration of critical reading into creative writing helps check the tendency to be influenced at second or third hand by writers whom one has not read, and broadens the field of *conscious* affiliations and repudiations available to each student's work. As I often remind my students, one can learn as much from seeing what one *doesn't* want to do as from discovering what one does want to do.

Form, like theory, is a resource, including the resource of restriction: the French poet and critic Paul Valéry wrote that the artist is he whose imagination is stimulated by constraints, and poetry is as much about what is not written as about what is. Whatever forms a student ultimately chooses for his or her own work, she should be aware of as many of the possibilities available to her as possible, and of the uses to which these have been put in the past and are being put now. Of course, in order for this to happen she or he must become aware of the active presence of form as such, and of its inescapability—as Eliot might have said, there is form that works and form that doesn't work, but there is never formlessness, just as true randomness always falls into patterns.

There is no single past or present of any artistic medium, but rather many, both coexisting and competing. It's the duty of every writer to maintain and expand rather than diminish the medium's formal capacities. It's the duty of every teacher of writing to make those capacities as available as possible to his or her students.

I try in my discussions to show students that reading critically and reading for pleasure are indissoluble or at least complementary, that the first leads to and enhances the second. When I read a poem, by a student, in a literary journal, in a collection of poems by a single author, or in an anthology, I *want* to enjoy the poem, to immerse myself in the poem's world. The problems that constructive criticism points out are impediments to that enjoyment, stumbling blocks to my attempt to enter the poem. Thus such criticism is in the service of pleasure: it aims to increase the reader's pleasure in the poem and the clarity and intensity of the experience that the poem provides. This doesn't mean that the poem must be pleasant in its subject matter or even in its techniques, but that it should provide the pleasure of a fully achieved aesthetic accomplishment, whatever its other aims. Nor does this preclude the possibility that a poem can and sometimes should be asked to try to accomplish more than it aims at, that a reader should expect it to provide a richer or deeper experience than its original conception proposes. As the brilliant poet and teacher Michael Anania once told me, one of the tasks of the creative writing instructor is to say, "You've done this very well. What else can you do?"

My creative writing courses emphasize the interdependence of writing and reading, stressing poetry as a practice of *language.* To misquote Mallarmé, poems are made out of words, not out of emotions (though words both entail and embody emotions). Poetry arises from the engagement with poetry; emulation and even imitation are an integral part of writing, as they are of so many other activities. Ezra Pound wrote that technique is the test of a writer's sincerity, while T. S. Eliot wrote that no verse is free for the writer who wants to do a good job. I try to remind students that in poetry language is not a means but an end; that language *itself* can speak, can tell us (including the writer) things we didn't already know. The poem can be a new experience in itself, not simply a commentary on experience.

Making reading and responding to reading central to the poetry workshop provides a common frame of reference and a common vocabulary, especially since even those students who have read some poetry have very rarely read the same poetry. Among other things, this can help students transform personal opinions into considered arguments, by providing a context for their thoughts and reactions. Instead of discussing "metaphor" in the abstract, for example, we can look at the ways Stevens uses metaphors as figures of thought and landscape in "Credences of Summer" or "The Snow Man." With undergraduates, who have usually read very little, my aim is to introduce them to conceptions of what a poem is and can be outside of the very limited models I have mentioned above. With graduate students, who often have a prematurely fixed view of the kinds of writers they are and the kinds of writing to which they are willing to respond, my aim is to encourage them to question their preconceptions by introducing them to work that challenges their assumptions of what poetry is or should be.

When having students read more complex or challenging work, I urge them to first allow themselves to *experience* it, immersing themselves in its language and its imagery, before irritably reaching after certainty—to postpone their will to understand or master the poem in favor of exploring the world that the poem offers. Just as in life we often have experiences whose impact is clear but whose meaning only becomes apparent later if at all, so is often the case in reading poems.

In my poetry workshops at least half of the students' poems are responses to assigned readings chosen on the basis of work that will expand their ideas of what is possible in poetry and of work that highlights specific aspects of writing poems (such as Stevens's embodiment of ideas in images, or Ann Lauterbach's use of syntax as a structural principle, or Carl Phillips's distanced, objectified treatment of personal material). I want students to think of the readings as a tool box from which they can draw techniques and resources for their own poems, and also to realize that they can make use of a poet's work (including by clarifying for themselves things they don't want to do) even if they don't necessarily "like" it (and that a second or third reading of a work may yield different impressions than a first glance will).

Such an engagement with *poems* (as distinct from an abstract notion of "poetry") can produce a sense of participation with poetry as a practice (a practice with a history as well as a present) and as a discipline, not simply as a mode of unconsidered or even self-conscious "self-expression." It can also help students realize that "self-expression" is a much more complex thing than it may at first appear, and that clichés and vagueness (not the same thing as ambiguity or clear and well-deployed abstraction) are obstacles to *any* accurate and effective expression. My larger aim is to steer students toward the production of aesthetic objects with an independent existence in the world.

Most students will not become professional writers, nor do most even aim at that. But such a heightened attention to language can make them better and more involved readers, and will improve all their writing, be it letters or academic essays or business reports. I also hope that it may at least help to make them less susceptible to the seductions of dead and false language that surround us in all areas of life and serve as impediments to actually living, as opposed to merely existing.

WORKS CITED

Bernstein, Charles, Ann Lauterbach, Jonathan Monroe, and Bob Perelman. "Poetry, Community, Movement: A Conversation." *Diacritics* 26.3–4 (1996): 196–210.

Fischer, Barbara K. "Into the Language Lab." *Boston Review,* March–April 2007.

Intention, Aspiration, Inspiration

On the Intentional Fallacy

One of the greatest legacies of the much-maligned (mainly by people who haven't really read them) New Critics is the separation of the author and the text. When I read a poem, I read the poem. I have neither the desire nor the ability to discern an author's intentions. I care about what the author *wrote,* not what the author thought he or she was writing. Even if one thinks of a work in terms of its author, if what mattered most to a writer was what was in his or her head, there'd be no reason to write anything, since one already has access to the contents of one's own mind. One writes because one wants to produce something separate from oneself. I can't imagine how I could fathom Shakespeare's intentions, for example, or how, if I could, that would usefully illuminate his plays. In Keats's words, the poet is no one.

To fully understand a Shakespeare play, if such a "full" understanding is ever possible, which is questionable, one must at the least understand what the words in the play meant at the time and to understand the literary, cultural, and historical allusions and references. If one doesn't know that the phrase "chimney-sweepers" in the lyric "Golden lads and golden girls all must / As chimney-sweepers, come to dust" from *Cymbeline* refers to dandelions, much of the passage's meaning will be missed, though its beauty remains even without its meaning. (Meaning isn't everything. Hugh Kenner, in *The Pound Era,* argues that, given our post-Symbolist modes of reading poetry, the resonance and evocativeness of the passage actually increase if one doesn't get the original reference, allowing the words and phrases to drift free of their original context into the realms of reverie.) But that is a matter of the text, not of the author. Understanding historical context is not the same thing as understanding the author or his intentions.

It is the then-public meanings of the words we are looking at that we are investigating when we look at an historical text and ask what a word "meant" at a given time. If an author is using a word in a purely idiosyncratic sense, that sense will either become clear in the textual context or the usage will simply be a stumbling-block. Even if an author tells us (in another text that is not the poem), "This is what I meant the word to mean," as Hart Crane did in his famous explication of "At Melville's Tomb" for *Poetry* founder Harriet Monroe, that will not make the word mean what he wants it to mean. If words are not public entities, then they are useless as a means of communication or even expression. The authorial explanation does not change the text, nor is the author necessarily the expert on his own text. The plethora of Shakespeare interpretations over the centuries has long outstripped any possible intentions Shakespeare could have had.

In Terry Eagleton's words (reviewing a book about that prolific author, "Anonymous"), "There is a difference between what *Middlemarch* is seeking to do at any particular point, and what George Eliot had in mind at the time, if she had anything particular in mind at all. The literary intentions that matter are those built into a work itself, rather as the structure of a chair 'intends' one's sitting on it." Whatever the author's intention, mine, yours, or Shakespeare's, if it's not manifested in the work it doesn't exist, not for a reader, not in any literary and not merely biographical sense. The work of art is, in part, an objectification of intention, and to the extent that the intention is objectified, it's no longer the author's. "The problem of intention arises from the fact that the author's declared [or private] intention as to his design or meaning are one thing, and his achieved intention—the actual intention or meaning framed within the work itself—quite another thing, even when the one and the other happen to agree or coincide" (Stallman 399).

I rarely sit down to write with a particular intention, except to write a good poem; I almost never sit down intending to write a poem on a particular topic, theme, or subject, though I sometimes have an idea of the kind of poem I want it to be, that is, of its formal shape. But even then, the poem usually takes its own direction. Words, phrases, lines, and images come to me, though obviously I work and rework the material given to me. In many of my poems I am assembling and manipulating lines and phrases I've accumulated over a period of time that seem to go together: writing the poem is my way of figuring out *how* they go together. It's often only after writing the poem, when I approach it as a reader, that I discover what it's "about" or, better, what is happening in it, how it works.

I'm sure every writer has had the experience, sometimes frustrating, often exhilarating, of the work taking off in a completely different direction than that which he or she "intended." As Jack Spicer said in his Vancouver lectures, you might start out wanting to write a poem about the Vietnam War and you end writing a poem about skating in Vermont. Perhaps other people's poems do what they tell them to, but mine rarely do. In any case, I trust the poem's intentions more than my own, because language knows better than I do, language knows more than I do. It's certainly been around longer than I have. As William Wimsatt and Monroe C. Beardsley, coiners of the phrase "the intentional fallacy," write in their famous essay of the same name, "The poem is not the critic's own and not the author's (it is detached from the author at birth and goes about the world beyond his power to intend about it or control it). The poem belongs to the public. It is embodied in language, the peculiar possession of the public, and it is about the human being, an object of public knowledge."

"Language, which permeates our minds and obeys not the laws of *things* but its own laws . . . has an organism's power to mutate and adapt and survive, and exacts obligations from us because no heritage is more precious" (Kenner 123). There's an intentionality to language, to the verbal work of art, because the accretion of previous writing conditions whatever new work is written, and the new work, in turn, modifies what comes before it, or at least the way that we read it. As Eliot writes in "Tradition and the Individual Talent," "What happens when a new work is created is something that happens simultaneously to all the works of art which preceded it. . . . The past [is] altered by the present as much as the present is directed by the past" (*Selected Prose* 38, 39). This also means that how and what a text speaks changes over time. But there are limits to that process, limits inherent in the text itself.

The fact that a poem doesn't embody authorial intention doesn't mean that it can't be misread, in the sense of misunderstanding the words and their relationships to one another, syntactic and semantic. When a student tells me that he thinks that Shakespeare's Sonnet 71 ("No longer mourn for me when I am dead / Than you shall hear the surly sullen bell / Give warning to the world that I am fled / From this vile world, with vilest worms to dwell") is spoken by a dog, he is not misreading the author's intention but misreading the actual words of the actual poem. Again, this is a question of the text, not of the author.

All language is intentional in the sense that the speaker intended to say *something*. Language is not a natural phenomenon, but the product of human thoughts and actions. Words do not appear on the page by accident, speech acts do not spontaneously generate themselves. This is both so obvious and so general as to be trivial. It tells us nothing about how to approach any given piece of language.

Intention does matter in the sense that the writer intended to put these words together in this order, and this combination of words has a denotative sense it is safe to assume was intended on the part of the author. But that's simply the fact of certain words in certain combinations meaning certain things and not other things. This doesn't take us very far in "reading" the poem in the sense of interpreting it (as Allen Grossman writes, decipherment is not understanding).

Different forms of discourse follow different sets of rules. In an essay (this essay, for example), a grant proposal, an instruction manual, or a love letter, intention is indeed crucial if not paramount: it's my intention to convey information or a point of view to a reader, and if I fail to do so, then the piece fails as writing. (This leaves aside the question of an audience misreading or misunderstanding the text.) Such writing is purposive, meant to achieve some goal—it is a means to an end. But to what end is a poem the means? (To see a poem as only the actualization or concretization of the author's intention is a functionalist view in which the text itself disappears: once the code is broken, the actual message is discarded.) Thinkers from Plato and Aristotle to Roland Barthes and Julia Kristeva agree that poetry is a different mode of discourse than expository or persuasive prose, though poetry can be written in prose as well as in verse, as Baudelaire and Mallarmé first demonstrated. There are of course didactic and even polemical poems, but a poem is hardly the most efficacious way to inform or persuade. The primary purpose of poems isn't to convey information, at least in that instrumental sense.

This extended passage from "The Intentional Fallacy" (from which I have quoted more briefly above) sums up very well the central questions of interpretation and intention:

> There is a difference between internal and external evidence for the meaning of a poem. And the paradox is only verbal and superficial that what is (1) internal is also public: it is discovered through the semantics and syntax of a poem, through our habitual knowledge of the language, through grammars, dictionaries, and all the literature which is the source of dictionaries, in general through all that makes a language and culture; while what is (2) external is private or idiosyncratic; not a part of the work as a linguistic fact: it consists of revelations (in journals, for example, or letters or reported conversations) about how or why the poet wrote the poem—to what lady, while sitting on what lawn, or at the death of what friend or brother. There is (3) an intermediate kind of evidence about the character of the author or about private or semiprivate meanings attached to words or topics by an author or by a coterie of which he is a member. The meaning of words is the history of words, and the biography of an author, his use of a word, and the associations which the word had for him, are part of the word's history and meaning. But the three types of evidence, especially (2) and (3), shade into one another so subtly that it is not always easy to draw a line between examples, and hence arises the difficulty for criticism. The use of biographical evidence need not involve intentionalism, because while it may be evidence of what the author intended, it may also be evidence of the meaning of his words and the dramatic character of his utterance. On the other hand, it may not be all this. (Wimsatt and Beardsley, 10–11)

If it were the case that one's primary goal in reading is to discern the author's intentions, one could and should simply bypass the text and go ask the author, if possible. But presumably the author writes in order to create things that are not himself or herself. "The evaluation of the work of art remains public; the work is measured against something outside the author" (Wimsatt and Beardsley, 10). I obsess over my poems in order to make them as close to perfect aesthetic objects as I can, not in order to make my "intentions" clear. A lot of writing for me is about swerving away from myself (a version of Eliot's escape from personality), about trying to connect to something outside of and beyond myself. I want my poems to exist independently of me, to be new objects in the world, like paintings or sculptures, not expressions of myself or my intentions. Obviously my self, my feelings, my thoughts, and, yes, my intentions are part of the material that makes up those objects. But if the poem is successful, they are just that: artistic material. If the poem is not successful, then it becomes a mere personal document. In that case, perhaps, authorial intention is the main interest, but that is the worst-case scenario. "Once the work is produced, it possesses objective status—it exists independently of the author and of his declared intention. It contains, insofar as it is a work of art, the reason why it is thus and not otherwise. The difference between art and its germinal event is absolute" (Stallman 399).

My interest in a poem isn't in the author (though certainly some authors have led lives that were interesting in themselves, sometimes more interesting than the work, in general we only care about an author's life because we care about the author's work), and an author's biography won't explain his or her work. If it does, that indicates a failure in the work: it's not fully realized if it needs to be completed by biography. In work that lasts, what lasts is what remains after things like the author's intentions have faded away. It's hard to fathom the intentions of the author(s) of *The Epic of Gilgamesh,* yet we can still read it, historical and textual lacunae and all.

The importance of intention for the author and the significance of intention for the reader are two entirely different things. However important his or her intention may be to the writer (it may be the whole reason he or she wrote the poem), that doesn't mean that it's important for a *reader.* While the writer may be full of intention, what the *reader* has is *text,* nothing more, nothing less. However one conceives of the text's relationship to its author, in relation to the reader the text must do all the work, has to give the reader everything he or she needs for a complete experience. If it needs to be supplemented by biographical information, it is to that extent a failed text. As Wimsatt and Beardsley write, "If the poet succeeded in doing it, then the poem itself shows what he was trying to do. And if the poet did not succeed, then the poem is not adequate evidence, and the critic must go outside the poem—for evidence of an intention that did not become effective in the poem" (4). The text is, or should be, a work of art, and it must be able to stand on its own in the world without the crutch of the author to support it, like a painting or a statue. To close with Wimsatt and Beardsley's words, "Judging a poem is like judging . . . a machine. [RS: William Carlos Williams called the poem a machine made out of words.] One demands that it work. It is only because an artifact works that we infer the intention of the artificer."

WORKS CITED

Eliot, T. S. *Selected Prose of T. S. Eliot.* Ed. Frank Kermode. New York: Farrar, Straus and Giroux, 1975.

Kenner, Hugh. *The Pound Era.* Berkeley: University of California Press, 1973.

Stallman, Robert W. "Intentions, Problem of." *Princeton Encyclopedia of Princeton and Poetics.* Enlarged ed.

Wimsatt, William, and Monroe C. Beardsley. "The Intentional Fallacy." *The Verbal Icon: Studies in the Meaning of Poetry.* University of Kentucky Press, 1954.

Some Thoughts on the Long Poem

1

I am much occupied with the question of the long poem and major poetry. It has always been my goal not just to be a poet but to be an important poet, to be a poet who matters. I've never seen the point of doing anything if one is only to be competent at best. Inevitably then, the question arises: Must one write a long poem in order to be an important poet, let alone to be a major poet? It seems these days that everyone is writing a long poem of some kind or another: a sense of project, of continuity, of writing by the book rather than by the poem, is *de rigeur* in certain circles. As Jasper Bernes, a former student, friend, and wonderful poet, has written, "We are in a historical moment . . . where the collection or miscellany of poems/writings has had its star dimmed by the long poem, the serial poem and [the] proceduralist or mixed-genre book." One is almost obligated to write not just poems but *books,* to have a project and preferably a system, although the project is often more engaging than the product. This moment parallels that of the mid- and late-nineteenth century, when it was incumbent upon every poet who aspired to major status to write a book-length poem, preferably an epic of one kind or another.

On the one hand, I have always longed toward the longer work, lusted after the architectonic sweep of "the major poem." While my attention span has lengthened (when I was a teenager I had trouble extending a poetic thought beyond a single line), I am still a sprinter rather than a long-distance runner. My arcs exhaust themselves, especially given my detailed attention to word set next to word. I envy those who can go the distance, who can stay in the race for page after page. On the other hand,

I'm suspicious of the American obsession with size. Bigger is not always better, as trade deficits, personal tragedies, or even daily irritations demonstrate, and concision is a virtue in any kind of discourse. Often in reading a long poem I think, "Were all these words really necessary?" I'm all too aware of the pages going by, each more slowly than the last, until I'm mired in the middle of a muddy track with no final goal post in sight. As Dr. Johnson said of *Paradise Lost,* no one ever wished it longer.

Perhaps one can say of the cult of the long poem what Adorno wrote of the nineteenth-century cult of the majesty of nature: "Such a cult is a reflex of the bourgeois delusion of grandeur, of the social preoccupation with quantities and record bests and also of bourgeois hero worship" (103), though of course the bourgeoisie did not invent either delusions of grandeur or hero worship.

Since the early nineteenth century, that is to say since Beethoven, the culture hero of classical music, the symphony has been regarded as the pinnacle of the composer's art. To be able to sustain a musical idea over the arc of a symphony has been the test of a great composer. For the arch-symphonist Mahler, greatness meant monumentality. But a symphony is not defined merely by length, but by its integral structure; it excludes the extraneous in a way that the tone poem, for example, does not. By this criterion, few modern and contemporary long poems would qualify.

However respected they may be, those who chose not to write symphonies, like Debussy, or who worked only on the small scale, like Satie, whose claims to unseriousness should not be taken seriously, or Webern, whose seriousness is not in doubt even among his detractors, are often regarded as somehow lesser, diminutive not just in the length of their productions. (Webern did write a piece he called a symphony: it lasts less than ten minutes.)

Debussy did, however, write an opera. From the 1700s, before Beethoven, through at least the 1930s, opera has exerted a magnetic pull on composers, and composing an opera can also stake one's claim to majority. This has especially been the case in the wake of Wagner, whose reinvention of opera almost displaced the symphony from its place at the pinnacle of the classical music hierarchy. Interestingly, while a single opera can suffice to accredit a composer as major (just as a single long poem, "when that long poem is good enough, when it has within itself the proper unity and variety" [Eliot, *On Poetry and Poets* 44], can credential one as a major poet: whatever their merits as poems, how many actually *read* Milton's *Paradise Regained* or *Samson Agonistes*?), one needs to have written more than one symphony for one's symphonizing to count toward major status. One needs not just to have composed a symphony, but to be a symphonist.

Why is a lyric poet so often considered "mere" when compared to a writer of the long poem? There is an element of the will to power in the will to write a long poem, a macho aspect (for both male and female poets) that's both alluring and repellent. In her poem "When I Buy Pictures," Marianne Moore admonishes that "nor may the / approved triumph easily be honored— / that which is great because something else is small." Writing a long poem, a book-length poem, proves that one can tough it out over the long haul; to be a writer of brief lyrics is a little wimpy, lacking in stamina. Some might consider the long poem to be patriarchal, authoritarian, an assertion of phallic power and domination. Thinking of the long poem as the attempt to take hold of a major theme, to make a major statement and stake one's claim on greatness, I'm reminded of Adorno's admonition: "It is silly to think that art can augment its dignity by dealing with some August event or other. More often than not this augustness is the upshot of an authoritarian ideology, specifically of respect for power and magnitude" (214–15). Viewed more positively, the will to write a long poem shows ambition and scope; the capacity to carry out that ambition shows determination and strength. In Milton's words, "Fame is the spur." But James Longenbach points out that, if done out of obedience to the necessities of the poem (some poems ask to be sonnets, some ask to be epics), rather than to the demands of the poet's ego, writing a long poem can be conceived of as an act of humility.

As Jasper Bernes puts it, more neutrally (and, probably, more fairly) than I have done, "Writing a wonderful poem turns out to be, in the end, not all that hard. . . . Producing an object that lies between two flaps, though, whether a collection or a 'book,' seems somehow, in my experience, more difficult." I am much less sanguine about the abundance, let alone the overabundance, of good poems, let alone of "wonderful poems," but I take Bernes's point that the short lyric can be seen as less demanding, of the writer and the reader, than the long poem. There remains the question of whether the long poem's demands justify themselves in the rewards that the poem yields, for either party. Bernes also acknowledges this question, without attempting to answer it: "The drawback to the popularity of the book over the collection is that the book's concept, idea, base may be used as an apology for . . . tedium without recourse to any of the arguments for the value of tedium."

Because I am not that kind of writer, or have not yet been that kind of writer (I can't predict the writer that I will be), the question troubles me. Is it a failing in me that I haven't written a long poem, that I proceed from poem to poem, that I don't have a *project*? Is the lack of such a project equivalent to the lack of a poetics? (I leave aside, for now, the question of what it would mean to "have" or "not have" a "poetics," or whether it's even possible not to have one of some sort or another, articulated or not.) And what about the possibility that the project replaces the poem, that, as so often happens, the idea overtakes the object, the text is read as intention rather than as aesthetic experience? Bernes's ruminations conclude with this admonition: "Let's not confuse the book with poetry, and let's not forget about the possibilities that the individual, and even [the] short, poem (or piece) offers—however much the weak minded have asked us to believe that such a notion is inherently bourgeois." (Perhaps because I've never been bourgeois or even close, it's never been clear to me what's so bad about it.)

2

In his essay "What Is Minor Poetry?" T. S. Eliot allows that a poet may be accounted major even if he or she has not written a long poem. In his words, "A work which consists of a number of short poems, even of poems which, taken individually, may appear rather slight, may, if it has a unity of underlying pattern, be the equivalent of a first-rate long poem in establishing an author's claim to be 'major'" (*On Poetry and Poets* 44). His example is George Herbert; another obvious example, to me if not to Eliot, would be Emily Dickinson. He also points out that we would consider John Donne a major poet even if he had never written his epistles and satires (indeed, those are probably the least-read of Donne's works), and would likewise so consider William Blake had he never written his prophetic books. But while Eliot writes that "the difference between major and minor poets has nothing to do with whether they wrote long poems, or only short poems," he goes on to say that "the *very* greatest poets, who are few in number [he names only Shakespeare and Milton], have all had something to say which could only be said in a long poem" (*On Poetry and Poets* 47).

Following on Eliot, Henry Gould points out that the long poem is not only a formal but also an intellectual construct. The long poem is one outcome (though not the only possible one) of what James Longenbach calls "the big hunger," the will to grapple with the largest possible questions. Mahler believed that the symphony should contain and/or construct an entire world. Many long poems seek to encompass or create a world, perhaps even *the* world.

While most poets considered major have written at least one long poem, to write a long poem, a book-length poem even, does not in itself suffice to make a poet major. Otherwise Edwin Arnold, author of *The Light of Asia* (a poem Eliot mentions with childhood fondness), would be a major poet. All that's required to write a long poem is endurance and a good dose of chutzpah. To write a *good* long poem, on the other hand, a poem worth the reader's investment of time, attention, and energy, is quite another matter. In Eliot's words, "It might seem at first simpler to refer to the minor writers of epics as *secondary,* or still more harshly as *failed great* poets. They have failed, certainly, in the sense that no one reads their long poems now: they are secondary, in the sense that we judge long poems according to very high standards. We don't feel that a long poem is worth the trouble unless it is, in its kind, as good as *The Faerie Queene,* or *Paradise Lost,* or *The Prelude,* or *Don Juan,* or *Hyperion,* and the other long poems which are in the first rank" (*On Poetry and*

Poets 41). To write a very long poem which is worth reading is undoubtedly a major accomplishment, even if it does not necessarily make one a major poet, but, again, to be a major poet doesn't mean that one must write a long poem worth reading.

As Eliot indicates, though, it is not necessarily the case that a long poem is what makes a major poet major, or even important. (I'm writing as much of reputation as of intrinsic quality: my focus is on what confers "majority" upon a poet.) While *In Memoriam* is undoubtedly a major work, it's not to *The Idylls of the King* that we turn when we turn to Tennyson. Browning's *The Ring and the Book* was always, I think, more admired than read, and now it is not even that. "The Man with the Blue Guitar," "Owl's Clover," and "Notes Toward a Supreme Fiction" (all of them long, none of them quite book-length) are all fine poems, though "Notes Toward a Supreme Fiction" is at moments discursively expository, and there are sing-songy aspects to "The Man with the Blue Guitar": "He held the world upon his nose / And this-a-way he gave a fling. // His robes and symbols, ai-yi-yi— / And that-a-way he twirled the thing." But it is not primarily for these poems that I, at least, treasure Wallace Stevens, though I adore "The Auroras of Autumn." Ezra Pound's debatable standing as an important poet rests much more on his short lyrics (and by no means even most of those) than on *The Cantos,* let alone on "Hugh Selwyn Mauberley" or *Homage to Sextus Propertius.* (His importance as a literary figure, an editor, theorist, and propagandist, is beyond question.) It's not because of *Paterson* that we read William Carlos Williams; indeed, that poem is hardly read in its entirety at all. Though H.D.'s *Trilogy* is full of lovelinesses, and attracted a great deal of attention at the time, largely due to its wartime themes, it's not now the basis of her reputation. (Considering the presence of lines like "Evil was active in the land, / Good was impoverished and sad: // Ill promised adventure, / Good was smug and fat," perhaps that's for the best.) Nor is her *Helen in Egypt,* though I am quite fond of it. But of the American Modernists and their immediate successors, few did not at least attempt a long poem, if not an epic of some kind: only Louise Bogan (wedded to "the stripped, still lyric" as she was), e. e. cummings, Robert Frost, and Marianne Moore come to mind.

Critic Joseph Conte writes that "the long poem has been the measure and the lifework of many significant 20th-century American poets. Yet the term *long poem* is a notoriously vague descriptor applied (by poets and critics alike) to poems of vastly different lengths and forms. One can discriminate, however, between those long poems in the 20th century that maintain the organizational structure of the epic and those that adopt the random and incomplete process of seriality. Epic poems by 20th-century poets adapt or renovate forms whose theoretical and structural underpinnings were set in earlier periods. The series, or serial poem, is remarkable for being the long form that is entirely new in 20th-century poetics" (283).

In his essay on Tennyson's *In Memoriam,* Eliot writes that "Tennyson's long poems are not long poems in quite the same sense as those of his contemporaries. They are very different in kind from *Sordello* or *The Ring and the Book. . . . Maud* and *In Memoriam* are each a series of poems. . . . *In Memoriam* is unique: it is a long poem made by putting together lyrics" ("'In Memoriam,'" *Selected Prose* 241, 243). If we conceive of the string of lyric poems comprising *In Memoriam* as a series (M. L. Rosenthal and Sally Gall consider the poem too discursive, too meditative, and too thematically consistent to qualify under their definition of a poetic sequence), or if we think further back to the sonnet sequences of the English Renaissance, from Sidney's *Astrophil and Stella* to Spenser's *Amoretti,* and not excluding Shakespeare's sonnets, I'm not sure how new the series or serial poem really can be said to be. Like Conte's postmodern serial poem, these also accede to flux and mutability; indeed, many take it as their topic. But Conte's schema, though too centered around the specific concerns and claims of his book *Unending Design: The Forms of Postmodern Poetry,* is still useful.

Conte also points out, in attempting to account for the turn toward different models of the long poem than the epic, that "the [failure] of several modernist epic poems to cohere or achieve their goals, including *The Cantos* and *Paterson,* and the distaste for the hierarchical structures and belief systems that frame them [I question this easy elision of forms and their significances, as I don't believe that forms have intrinsic meanings] has led many postmodern poets to serial composition" (285). Conte also notes the discontent with and restlessness within the confines of the short poem that Jasper Bernes discusses: "Poems written in many loosely associated parts also signify the impatience of poets with the short personal lyric" (285). Jack Spicer, with his method of composition by the book and his dismissal of the individual poem, exemplifies this impatience. Rejecting his early work, Spicer writes to Donald Allen that "the poems belong nowhere. They are one night stands filled (the best of them) with their own emotions, but pointing nowhere, like sex in a Turkish bath." Spicer also writes that "there is really no single poem. . . . Poems should echo and reecho against each other. They should create resonances. They cannot live alone any more than we can."

In somewhat different and strikingly broader terms, for M. L. Rosenthal and Sally Gall, the genre they call the modern poetic sequence is "*the* modern poetic form within which all the tendencies of more than a century of experiment define themselves and find their aesthetic purpose. . . . The sequence has been [our major poets'] great vehicle for discovering the full possibilities of dynamic interplay among poems and fragments conceived under the same ultimate psychological pressure or creative impulse" (vii). Rather than being organized narratively or thematically, the modern poetic sequence is based on what they call lyrical structure: "The modern poetic sequence, then, is a grouping of mainly lyric poems and passages, rarely uniform in pattern, which tend to interact as an organic whole. It usually includes narrative and dramatic elements, and ratiocinative ones as well, but its structure is finally lyrical. Intimate, fragmented, self-analytical, open, emotionally [and intellectually and formally] volatile, the sequence meets the needs of modern sensibility even when the poet aspires to tragic or epic scope" (9). Rosenthal and Gall cite Whitman's *Song of Myself* as the first modern poetic sequence, but also look back to Tennyson's *Maud,* though in their view that poem does not quite shake off the constraints of plot: it occupies "the very meeting point of long poem and sequence" (19).

If Conte's categorization seems too arbitrarily restrictive,

Rosenthal and Gall's seems overly capacious. Though they make a (not very clearly defined) distinction between the long poem and the poetic sequence, every extended poem of the last hundred years or so, or set of poems that is not strictly and solely narrative, even every book of poems that can in some way be seen as linked or unified, qualifies as a modern poetic sequence, whether so presented or not (though their rather hefty book includes no mention of Oppen or Zukofsky, nor of masterpieces of black modernism like Langston Hughes's *Montage of a Dream Deferred* or Melvin B. Tolson's *Harlem Gallery*). They sweep so much into their category—including Dickinson's fascicles, Housman's *A Shropshire Lad,* Yeats's *Words for Music Perhaps,* Edgar Lee Masters's *Spoon River Anthology, The Waste Land, The Cantos, Paterson,* Stevens's "The Auroras of Autumn," Muriel Rukeyser's *Elegies,* Basil Bunting's *Briggflatts,* David Jones's *The Anathemata,* Geoffrey Hill's *Mercian Hymns,* Lowell's *Life Studies* and *Day by Day,* Berryman's *77 Dream Songs,* Ginsberg's *Kaddish,* Sylvia Plath's last poems, Ted Hughes's *Crow,* Galway Kinnell's *The Book of Nightmares,* and many individual poems that are only a few pages long—that it loses all descriptive value. It's hard to see what all these very different works share besides taking up more than a few pages.

4

It seems to me that there are three ways to proceed into and through a longer poem. Though in a different context altogether, the critic and poet James Longenbach has summed them up well: "We know how to move forward depending on the syntax we employ, and if the word 'because' puts one foot purposefully in front of the other, if the word 'and' permits us to wander, the word 'or' forces us to stagger" (83). I would say that "because" corresponds to narrative, something following from something in a line, however curved or crooked: in E. M. Forster's example, the king died and the queen died of grief. The word "or" corresponds to digression, casting out and circling back: the king died in his sleep, or a tornado struck city hall, or the day of his death was a cold dark day, or somewhere someone had lamb stew for lunch, or I can't remember what I meant to say, but I'm sure it had something to do with the king: wasn't lamb his favorite meat? "And" would correspond to segmentation, the poem in sections, the serial poem, this and then this and then this: the king died one Saturday at noon, and the queen died on Monday at three, and the bells rang all weekend and then rang all week, and the day of the king's funeral was rainy and in the fifties, and several of the courtiers caught cold and were bedridden, and the day of the queen's funeral was not that same day, and the castle was painted green except in those spots painted blue. Unless they were yellow. Both digression and seriality or segmentation are variations of what Longenbach has called disjunction.

So here are the three modes by which to move and be moved through the long poem. There is narrative, raveling the thread of story (the word "ravel" means both to wind and to unwind), finding our way out of the labyrinth or feeling our way deeper within, hoping that there's an Ariadne at the end of the thread, or at least an interesting minotaur. (As Bugs Bunny says in his hairdresser persona, "In my line of work you meet lots of *interesting* people, but the most *interesting* ones are always the monsters.") Narrative is the oldest mode of the long poem, threading from *The Epic of Gilgamesh* and unspooling in various forms through *The Iliad, The Odyssey, The Aeneid, The Divine Comedy, The Faerie Queene* (these last two are as much philosophical allegories as stories in verse), *Paradise Lost,* and so on and on and on. Wordsworth's *The Prelude* may be considered as a psychological narrative, with plentiful digressions, the story of the creation of a consciousness. (Indeed, Wordsworth can be thought of as having invented subjectivity as a subject for English-language poetry.) Though it seems that almost every Anglophone poet in the nineteenth century attempted a book-length narrative of some sort or another, the long narrative has been considerably less popular since the advent of the Modernists. One might fit James Merrill's Ouija board epic, *The Changing Light at Sandover,* which digresses within a strongly narrative frame, here. Vikram Seth's 1986 *The Golden Gate,* momentarily popular as a novelty item, is a three-hundred-page verse novel about San Francisco Bay Area yuppies.

While finding one's way in and/or out of the labyrinth can sometimes be exhilarating—the thrill of meeting the minotaur a revelation (if one survives), Ariadne's kiss a rapture—in my reading experience too often the narrative poem just leaves one with a handful of used string, not good for much of anything and of no interest in itself. Here I am, at the heart of the labyrinth or at its door, and what do I do now? Perhaps we've simply been through too many labyrinths by now: the thrill of winding up that spool of string is gone. As Rosenthal and Gall write, "It is sheer dogmatism to rule out any form or genre as obsolete ('the novel is dead'), and it is always possible that some genius will find a way of writing a long, continuous narrative poem or logically or thematically organized one that will satisfy the most knowledgeable and sensitized of contemporary readers. But a fatal ennui with such efforts does seem to have set in, and not even the gifts of a poet as truly remarkable as Wallace Stevens have been able to achieve more than a momentary, suspect remission" (6).

Digression is another way to proceed, dropping one thought to pick up another, beginning and then beginning again, but always on some trail or another, leading to another trail and so forth. *Flow Chart,* by John Ashbery, our supreme poet of progression by digression, is the perfect, and perfectly lengthy, contemporary example. Digression ultimately derives from Freudian free association and Joycean stream of consciousness. The assumption is that there is some significance (in both senses of the word) to the elements that come to the mind and the order and manner in which they do so. Otherwise, it's just rambling and blathering, like that of a senile grandparent. The pleasure of digression is wandering and stumbling upon, as in the Surrealist calculated drift through unfamiliar urban neighborhoods in the hope of happening upon what Walter Benjamin called profane illuminations, or the Situationist *dérive,* noticing how certain areas, streets, or buildings resonate with states of mind and desires. *I wonder as I wander.*

The pleasures of getting lost are balanced against those of finding one's way home. When it fails, digression can feel pointless and aimless (activity is not action), an extended getting nowhere: true randomness is always boring, as is the willed wackiness so common in contemporary poetry. To misquote Longenbach quoting the psychoanalyst D. W. Winnicott, if it is a joy to be lost, it is a disaster not to be found. As Adorno writes in *Aesthetic Theory,* "'Origin and destination are the same': if there is any truth in this statement at all, then it must be in the field of art" (98).

Even if you retrace your steps and take a different branching of the road, you're never making the same trip twice. Beginnings are always the most exciting part of a journey, the parts most full of promise and surprise. Stay with them too long and the promises are either broken or prove stultifying (is *that* what I wanted?), the surprises stale (oh, *that* again). But to travel by veering, to move forward sideways, to wander and see what you stumble across (best to walk slowly, you might miss something on the way, or at least miss your footing)—that's always an adventure.

Another way into and through the extended poem, the most popular in our age of distraction and the short attention span, is to break the journey into stages, to take several journeys at once: the serial poem or poetic sequence, the poem in sections, some of which follow, some of which are simultaneous in time or place or both, some in different voices, some different perspectives on the same object, looking at it in the round. Many of the longer poems I admire are made up of accretions, constellations, series or sequences of smaller units, rather like life, in which we never see the whole picture, are never told the entire story. (What omniscient narrator could tell us that, even if we were around after our own deaths to hear it?) Ideally, their collocation forms a gestalt, a result greater than the sum of its parts.

Critic Alan Golding suggests that works like Robert Creeley's *Pieces* or *A Day Book,* book-length poems shying away from the large-scale or the major, exemplify the serial poem as a log of dailiness, both notating moment-to-moment attention and investigating the nature of that attention. Embracing the banal and the trivial, they thus evince modesty rather than ambition. The emphasis on a successive or sequential momentariness calls to mind these words of Jack Spicer's from his Vancouver Lectures: "Robin Blaser once said in talking about a serial poem that it's as if you go into a room, a dark room, the light is turned on for a minute, then it's turned off again, and then you go into a different room where a light is turned on and turned off" (Allen and Tallman 233). Many serial poems comprise, or aspire to comprise, such a sequence of momentary illuminations.

At its best, the poetic sequence or serial poem is an elastic and capacious mode, incorporating fragmentation and condensation, and the intensities usually associated with the brief lyric, within a larger though nonlinear arc, producing a rhizomatic art of subterranean networks and submerged connections. When it succeeds, it illuminates or even creates connections among disparate, often seemingly unrelated elements, producing a new gestalt. When such a poem is unsuccessful, the elements just pile up like dirty dishes or bills one doesn't want to open, or like one of those endless lines of traffic lights each of which turns red just as you get to it: one damned thing after another—again, like life at its most tedious. Conte writes that "the series is an ongoing process of accumulation," but seriality can feel like mere listing, the mere accumulation of things that multiply but don't add up, this and then this and then this *ad nauseam.*

For Joseph Conte there is something new under the poetic sun, and it is the serial poem. Though I question Conte's claims for its uniqueness or special suitability to our times, almost all of what are considered the major long poems of the Modernist period and beyond are serial or at least segmental in form and procedure. Though Conte accounts *The Cantos* as epic and not serial, on ideological rather than aesthetic grounds, and with Mussolini trotted out for sensationalist effect, the poem is clearly serial in form. Perhaps works like *The Cantos* and H.D.'s *Trilogy* and *Helen in Egypt,* among others, might call for a new category of the serial epic. Conte cites such diverse examples of the serial poem as Williams's *Spring and All,* which mixes verse with rather skewed prose essays on poetry and the imagination, George Oppen's *Discrete Series* (though published as his first volume, it takes up only ten pages in the second volume of the Library of America's *American Poetry: The Twentieth Century*), and open-ended series such as Nathaniel Mackey's "Song of the Andoumboulou" and "mu," Rachel Blau DuPlessis's *Drafts,* and Robert Duncan's "Passages" (I would add "The Structure of Rime"), which are not bound within the confines of any single book. Many more examples of the modern and contemporary serial or segmented poem could be adduced, though I will not do so here. Suffice it to say they are sufficient to the day.

5

And so I return to the questions with which I began. Is it necessary for a poet to write a long poem to be a major, an important poet? And why is there such a strong perceived connection between length and importance?

My sometime ambitions and my habits and tastes are somewhat at odds with one another. I ask myself, "Why do you want to write a long poem when you don't in general want to read long poems? Is it sheer envy of the boys (and girls) with bigger toys?" Neither as a writer nor as a reader am I an exponent of the long poem. In general I find the experience of reading a long poem burdensome; it wearies me. My commitment is to the numinous lyric. I am an adherent of Keats's directive that the poet load every rift with ore, but it's impossible for the extended lode of the long poem, at least of a through-composed long poem, to be all gold. In "The Philosophy of Composition," Edgar Allan Poe denies the possibility of the long poem, which he holds to be at best a series of short poems strung together. (This is an accurate description of at least one species of the genus "serial poem." Hart Crane said that *The Bridge* was not an epic, but a "long lyric poem, with interrelated sections.") T. S. Eliot questions this view in his essay "From Poet to Valéry," in which he points out that the parts of a long poem "can form a whole which is more than the sum of its parts; a whole such that the pleasure we derive from the reading of any part is enhanced by our grasp of the whole. It follows also that in a long poem some parts may be deliberately planned to be less 'poetic' than others: these passages may show no luster when extracted, but may be intended to solicit, by contrast, the significance of other parts, and to unite them into a whole more significant than any of the parts. A long poem may gain by the widest possible variations of intensity. But Poe wanted a poem to be of the first intensity throughout" (*To Criticize the Critic* 34).

To return to the musical comparison, the "less poetic" parts of a long poem may be compared to operatic recitative, less immediately thrilling than the big showpiece arias, but necessary to place and set off those arias. An opera that was all arias would grow exhausting. Strauss's *Salome* and, even more, *Elektra* come close, but both are very short by operatic standards. And yet, a poem hits one less viscerally than music; one is more able to modulate and moderate its impact. Hearing a good live performance of "In Questa Reggia" from Puccini's *Turandot,* one's body *vibrates* with the force of the voice.

Thus rightly rebuked, I might view my stance as a limitation turned into principle: this is how Eliot views Poe's position. On the other hand, in the same essay Eliot writes that "the poet's theories should arise out of his practice rather than his practice out of his theories" (42). So perhaps I am not so far astray after all.

Wallace Stevens captures some of this ambivalence in a letter to Harriet Monroe, though he ultimately comes down in favor of the long poem (and affirms the requirement of variety that Eliot invokes), not for the sense of major accomplishment some take it to represent (he explicitly dismisses that), but for the unexpected or otherwise unavailable possibilities and potentialities it offers: "I have no desire to write a great deal. I know that people judge one by volume. However, having elected to regard poetry as a form of retreat, the judgment of people is neither here nor there. The desire to write a long poem or two is not obsequiousness to the judgment of people. On the contrary, I find that this prolonged attention to a single subject has the same result that prolonged attention to a senora has according to the authorities. All manner of favors drop from it. Only it requires a skill in the varying of the serenade that occasionally makes one feel like a Guatemalan when one particularly wants to feel like an Italian" (230).

Raising once again the question of how one defines a long poem (how long is long?), *The Waste Land,* an epic with all the boring bits left out, and the only "long poem" I count among my favorites, is about the longest poem that I can hold in my head more or less at once. And is it "really" a book-length poem? Eliot had to pad it out with notes, fascinating though they are, to fill a printed volume. Certainly in scope and range it must be accounted major: whatever Eliot's demurrals, it seeks to respond to the condition of an era.

The long poem is a relative concept, both in terms of sheer size and in terms of type. Is *X* "long," being only, say, twenty pages? Is *Y* a single poem, made up as it is of many distinct units? Often the difference between a collection of poems and a long poem is a matter of presentation: a set of lyrics can be strung together into a serial poem no more ambitious or capacious than the standard poetic miscellany. In positive terms, this is the long poem as an accretion of parts also readable in themselves as short lyrics or brief lyric sequences (many serial poems are broken down into sets of smaller serial units).

At an AWP panel on the modern poetic sequence in which I participated, an audience member asked how one distinguishes the long poem and the poetic sequence. To my mind, the difference lies in the degree of explicitness of the poem's unifying principle. The traditional long poem presents its principle of unity explicitly, either in narrative or thematic or intellectual terms. In the poetic sequence, the unifying principle is more submerged or even concealed (and sometimes absent altogether). The reader must discover or construct what unifies the poetic sequence in the experience of reading it.

Despite its moments of luminous intensity, I'd trade *The Cantos* for *Cathay,* though there are several individual Cantos I'd keep if I could, among them I, II, IV, XVII, and CXX, with its paradoxically beautiful confession of poetic failure. This brings up another aspect of the serial poem, its tendency to fissure into discrete lyrics with all the force and presence of free-standing poems. The serial poem is endlessly excerptable. The poems embedded in Williams's *Spring and All* are better known individually than as parts of a rather incoherent whole, and lose nothing when read separately. Zukofsky's *A* 11 can satisfy almost endlessly ("River that must turn full after I stop dying / Song, my song, raise grief to music / Light as my love's thought"). The serial poem frequently raises the question, "*Why* are these parts linked together? What larger whole do they comprise? *Is* the whole greater than the sum of its parts?"

It's not for *The Age of Anxiety* that I read Auden, though I'm quite fond of *The Sea and the Mirror,* a series of lyrics ("My Dear

One is mine as mirrors are lonely") and one prose meditation (Caliban's, of course) strung together to build an arc, one heavily dependent upon Shakespeare's *Tempest.* It's only for some of *The Dream Songs,* a serial poem if ever there was one, though not, I believe, discussed by Conte, that I read Berryman; "The Ball Poem" is probably my favorite work of his. But I am taken by "Homage to Mistress Bradstreet." At sixteen pages in his *Collected Poems,* including notes, does it count as "a long poem"? And then there are the many poets I love, from Sir Thomas Wyatt and Thomas Campion to Paul Celan and Osip Mandelstam, who never wrote a long poem at all, never even tried. I've never wished a Lorine Niedecker poem longer, and not for lack of love.

Thus I conclude with equivocations instead of stands, questions and conundrums rather than answers, preferences and predilections in place of positions.

WORKS CITED

Adorno, Theordo. *Aesthetic Theory.* Trans. C. Lenhardt. New York: Routledge and Kegan Paul, 1984.

Allen, Donald M., and Warren Tallman, eds. *Poetics of the New American Poetry.* New York: Grove, 1973.

Conte, Joseph. "Long and Serial Poetry." *The Facts on File Companion to 20th Century American Poetry.* Ed. Burt Kimmelman. New York: Facts on File, 2005.

Eliot, T. S. *On Poetry and Poets.* New York: Farrar, Straus and Cudahy, 1957.

Eliot, T. S. *To Criticize the Critic and Other Essays.* Ed. Thomas Stearns. New York: Farrar, Straus and Giroux, 1965.

Eliot, T. S. *Selected Prose of T. S. Eliot.* Ed. Frank Kermode. New York: Farrar, Straus and Giroux, 1975.

Longenbach, James. *The Resistance to Poetry.* Chicago: University of Chicago Press, 2004.

Rosenthal, M. L., and Sally Gall. *The Modern Poetic Sequence: The Genius of Modern Poetry.* New York: Oxford University Press, 1983.

Stevens, Wallace. *Letters of Wallace Stevens.* Ed. Holly Stevens. Berkeley: University of California Press, 1966.

In a Major Key

Like Stephen Spender, I think continually of those who are truly great. I strive to write work that lives up to theirs, while always fearing that it doesn't, that it may never attain those heights.

It's clear to me that some poets are more important than others. The world is awash with poets who have no reason to be writing, who make no difference to the world at large or to the world of poetry. I'm not referring to the outright bad poets, but to the sea of depressingly competent poets of no consequence, though sometimes of undeserved reputation. Richard Strauss supposedly said, "I may not be a first-rate composer, but I'm a first-rate second-rate composer." While I both admire his clear-eyed self-evaluation and recognize the boast within it, I am not so sanguine. I want to be a poet who matters and I want to read poets who matter. I want to be first-rate.

Some might say that dividing poets into major and minor is presumptuous or arrogant. This is a fair charge, but we all do this whether we admit it or not. We all decide that some poets are more important than others, although we may not articulate it in those terms. Listing one's favorite poets is often, though not always, a version of this ranking process. Who doesn't think that his or her favorite poets are better, are more important, than the poets he or she doesn't like?

A word like "major" always implies comparison, whether explicit or implicit, to its opposite, whether one calls that other "minor" or something else. The distinction, how it is to be made and what it means, troubles me. I worry about making it, and I worry about not making it. By T. S. Eliot's criteria in his essay "What Is Minor Poetry?" almost every poet who ever wrote is a minor poet. (In my heart I wonder, "Would I be among them?" and fear the answer.) As Mae West reputedly said, goodness has nothing to do with it. For Eliot, poetic excellence is a necessary condition for poetic majority, but hardly a sufficient one. I wouldn't want to emulate his sweeping judgments, especially because much more poetry matters to me than seems to have mattered to him. But still, the question haunts me, perhaps only because of my own personal ambitions as a poet (which are not the same as my poetic ambitions as a poet).

When reading a poem, a selection of poems, a book of poems, I ask myself, "Is this interesting? Is this engaging? Is this individual? Is this distinctive?" I frequently ask myself, "Is this worth reading? Was it worth writing?" Too often the answer to all these questions is "No." So much work has no reason for existing besides that the poet could, and presumably wanted to, write it. That's not enough if one is going to present the work to the world. I write in part for the dead, for the poets who made me want to be a poet, placing little votive gifts on their altars, hoping that my offering will be acceptable. I think it's more acceptable than most, but most poets don't even try for that. They write for themselves and their coteries.

Despite the spell that Eliot can cast on me, I don't ask myself when reading a poem or book of poems, "Is this major?" I do think, when I read some of the people who've most inspired me, like Keats or Stevens or Eliot, "This is great poetry." It would be more accurate to say that I think of some poetry as great than that I think of some poetry as major. But while my college mentor Alvin Feinman made a point of only reading great poetry, I am not so pure or so high-minded. I read, enjoy, and learn from much poetry, both of the past and of the present, that I wouldn't think of as great. And there is some great poetry I can't bear at all.

The question of whether something is of major accomplishment (which isn't equivalent to "of major length") is one I ask much more of my own poetry than of others' poetry. I want to do my best, but I know that sometimes one's best just isn't good enough. My ambition from the time that I began writing was to be a great poet. I haven't gotten there, but I still have hopes. At the same time, given the changes in the cultural climate and the role of art in general, and poetry in particular, I wonder if such a term even has any meaning anymore, or if it does, what that meaning is. Poetic greatness may not be simply a matter of individual accomplishment but of social context, a social context that no longer exists, and perhaps never existed in America. But my doubts and my questions don't erase the aspiration to greatness, even if it is impossible or no longer possible.

As Irish poet Mark Granier points out, a major poem is one that opens up new possibilities, breaks new ground in some way or another. It's a poem that creates ripples in the river of time, perhaps something like the stone in the stream in Yeats's "Easter 1916," momentarily halting the flow, or at least forcing it to bend, to accommodate itself to an object that won't be moved and can't be ignored. Henry Gould, in a comment on my long poem post (on "Reginald's Shepherd's Blog," January 24, 2007), also mentions a thematic ambition, an attempt to take hold of some larger topic or idea. *The Waste Land* certainly qualifies on both counts. But a great poem need not be major in scale. Emily Dickinson's "After great pain, a formal feeling comes" is a great poem, and it's only thirteen lines long.

When measured against the world, let alone against the universe, any individual is insignificant, though I don't think that diminishes the value of individual lives. My recognition of my own insignificance fuels my writing: I want my poetry to mitigate that insignificance. I try to write work that will be remembered. Whether one's work is remembered also depends on much that has nothing to do with its merit. Reading an article in *The Writer's Chronicle* about a public library in Fairfax, Virginia, that's discarding all books not checked out in the past two years, including literary classics, doesn't give one much hope for the possibility of literary immortality. No longer can one count on one's book sitting on the shelf waiting for the right reader, sleeping in the library until awakened by a reader's kiss.

Sometimes I wonder why I care, since I won't be around to know whether I'm being remembered. I don't believe in an afterlife, but if there were one, I suspect that I'd have other things with which to occupy myself than worrying whether people were reading my poetry. Unless the afterlife is like that in the recent novel *The Brief History of the Dead* by Kevin Brockmeier, in which people continue after their deaths so long as someone remembers them, and fade away when they're forgotten. In the novel, to be remembered indirectly doesn't count, but a poem, or a book of poems, allows one to live on in the minds of people one has never met. However one defines it, to be remembered is the only immortality we can have.

Taking Dictation from a Martian Muse

Jack Spicer's notion of poetry as dictation is hardly original (and originality is a notion Spicer would quarrel with in any case), but Spicer acknowledges its sources and rings his own changes on them: Yeats's spooks bringing him metaphors for his poetry, or Cocteau's Orphée writing down poems broadcast on the ghost radio. That the idea of dictation can itself be read as dictated makes perfect sense. Part of the point of Spicer's poetics is that everything comes from the outside; there's no romantic interiority generating poems in the sensitive soul. This is a useful corrective to the fetishization of personal creativity, proposing instead what Robin Blaser calls the practice of outside. As Spicer writes of his posthumous collaboration with García Lorca, "It was a game made out of summer and freedom and a need for a poetry that would be more than the expression of my hatreds and desires. It was a game like Yeats' spooks or Blake's sexless seraphim" (*After Lorca*).

I like the idea of poetry as dictation, because writing does feel like that sometimes. I've had at least one poem that was literally dictated to me—I woke up and the poem was reciting itself in my head, though I had to come up with my own ending. Don't we all? In that sense Spicer conveys what it often feels like to do poetry. The recent history of the study of the mind, from Freud's discovery/invention of the unconscious to breakthroughs in the biochemical understanding of the brain, certainly supports the idea of dictation, from some source or another. It has certainly revealed just how little of what we think or do is really under our control, though that's a pretty old idea dressed up in some new clothes. For the ancient Greeks, after all, the poet was a person possessed by a daimon, which is one of the reasons that Plato distrusted poets: they were not ruled by reason.

I also admire Spicer's ambition to make poems out of real objects, to "put the real cliff and the real ocean into the poem," and his conception of words as what sticks to the real, though I don't think that's possible, except to the extent that words are real objects out of which we build real poems. Language is a thing in the world as well as a thing about (in both senses) the world. Poetry, at least in part, is made out of the attempt to achieve that identity between word and world even while knowing that such a goal is unattainable. If you don't try, you're just playing games, doing parlor tricks (what Eliot meant when he said that poetry was a sophisticated diversion—luckily, he was lying). If you don't realize that it's impossible, then you end up with religion or dogma. Allen Grossman speaks of poetry as an impossible goal that every poem tries to achieve. If only every poem did so try! That dovetails with what Spicer writes that he learned from Robert Duncan, "not to search for the perfect poem [which doesn't and can't exist except as an aspiration] but to let your way of writing of the moment go along its own paths, explore and retreat but never be fully realized (confined) within the boundaries of one poem." That seems to balance the exploratory, experimental impulse with the recognition that failure is inevitable, that judgments still can and must be made. There are, after all, greater and lesser degrees of realization.

Interesting and even inspiring though Spicer's notion of dictation is, with its promise of escaping what he calls "the big lie of the personal," I wonder if it's not simply the mirror image of romantic inspiration. Instead of coming from deep within one, from one's soul or innermost self, the poem comes from outside one, from the Martians or the spooks. In either case, the poet is passive, and abdicates thought and responsibility. He listens for the nothing that is not there and the nothing that is. This can be seen as a kind of askesis, an emptying out of the self so that some Other can occupy that space, if only temporarily. It can also be seen as an evasion, since no one truly has the mind of winter of Stevens's snow man, at one with what surrounds him. Spicer's Martians seem to be the Muses dressed up in space suits, another way to preserve the romantic (small "r") notion of the poet as a specially inspired individual with access to the transcendent, and to preserve both the notion that there is a transcendent (Derrida's transcendental signifier?) out there waiting to be tapped into and the confidence that it can be reached. As Spicer insists in his Vancouver lectures, there is "a difference between you and the outside of you which is writing poetry," but the poet is still the radio. Not everyone receives these transmissions, after all. Capital "R" Romanticism, in its various incarnations, too often betrays the transcendent by identifying the poet's inspiring genius with his or her ego.

We ourselves are the real, part of a reality and a reality in ourselves. (Are we ourselves?, as The Fixx asked in song long ago.) That desire to connect with something outside us is also a desire to connect with something inside us (and vice versa—the way in is the way out, as Heraclitus might have said). We are part of what we see and talk about, but we are also inaccessible to ourselves in the same way and to the same degree that the "real world" is inaccessible to us. This idea of an internal and inaccessible real, an internal transcendent, is very Lacanian: for Lacan, the always lost Real is the level of immediate and unitary somatic experience, absent lack and lacking absence, from which language inevitably and necessarily alienates us. It is literally unspeakable.

So poetry is both about eroding boundaries and borders and about recognizing borders and boundaries that were invisible, and the poem isn't a representation of the world but an analogy of it. The materials out of which the poem is built (words, sounds, images, lines, phrases) are analogous to the materials out of which the world is made (bricks and rocks and twigs and leaves and mites and midges). If words are objects in the same way that bricks are, with their own heft and palpability, then that is the way (the one possible way) to make poems out of real objects. Analogy is one of Spicer's favorite words, and one of Stevens's.

The poem, when it is at its best, when we are at our best, is a kind of agon between the poet and the language, and the poet has to bring all his or her resources to bear, or it's not a real struggle at all, just a performance. After all, Stevens did say that the poem has to resist the intelligence almost successfully. For that resistance to be meaningful, the pressure of the intelligence must be strong. As Spicer notes, "The more you know . . . the more building blocks the Martians have to play with." Perhaps in reaction against Modernist "intellectualism," too many American poets from the 1940s onward (beginning with the generation of Lowell and Bishop and Jarrell) have surrendered or renounced their intelligence, which too often has resulted in taking dictation not from the Martians but merely from the culture at large, or (as too often) small. But poetry demands better listening than that.

Illness, Identity, and Poetry

Illness and Poetry

A Few Reflections

My friend the poet and critic Christopher Hennessy, who maintains a fascinating blog on the multiple relationships between identity (particularly gay identity) and creativity at *Outside the Lines,* recently asked me, after I described to him one of my chemotherapy side effects, that even picking up a piece of cold fruit burns my hands, whether I planned to write about the experience of having cancer and undergoing chemotherapy. Some excellent poetry has come out of that experience, most notably the late L. E. Sissman's *Hello Darkness.* The very much alive Marilyn Hacker has a fourteen-poem sequence called "Cancer Winter" in her book *Winter Numbers,* dealing with her experience of breast cancer. There is also, in prose, the late cultural critic Susan Sontag's *Illness as Metaphor* and, more problematically, *AIDS and Its Metaphors,* and the late Audre Lorde's *Cancer Journal.* I have not encountered the stigmatization of cancer Sontag writes of, though I am very familiar with the stigmatization of HIV, which has absorbed much of the "you brought this on yourself" discourse that used to surround cancer.

I've been fortunate in that I've encountered very little overt or subtle HIV stigma or homophobia in my adventures in the

---

Editor's Note: Shepherd completed "Illness and Poetry" in early March 2008. At that point, chemotherapy treatment had been successfully treating his cancer. The further surgery to come mentioned in section 3 refers to a surgical procedure called "radiofrequency ablation," which was successfully performed later in March and involved inserting a probe to burn up two tumors in his liver.

medical system, though both, along with racism, have reared their ugly heads on occasion, as when a nephrologist in upstate New York who hadn't even read my charge, after explaining to me that I was inevitably going to die of kidney failure, asked how I got HIV, because "you people" are very susceptible to a variety of nephritic necrosis that afflicts inner-city IV drug users (of all races—I'd looked it up). I explained that I was not an inner-city IV drug user, and immediately switched nephrologists, even though it meant traveling to Pennsylvania. I've been especially surprised not to have encountered more such prejudice down here in Pensacola, capital of the Redneck Riviera, except when a doctor wearing a cross ring asked how long I had been HIV. I explained that I was not a virus but a person living with a virus. He also, when asking whether I drank, misheard my reply that I didn't but that my partner and I sometimes cooked with wine to say that we had coke (as in cocaine) with wine. I didn't go back to him either.

But then, though I didn't think I could live here before we moved here, Pensacola is one of the only places I've ever lived where I've never even heard the word "nigger," though I did momentarily forget the bumper sticker I saw on a car in the local Winn-Dixie supermarket parking lot: "Keep 'em in the closet—Vote Republican." Clever, but more than a bit disturbing.

But, getting back to Christopher Hennessy's question, I don't plan to write much poetry about my experiences as a cancer patient, though one can never predict what will come to one. Although the experience is very wearing, very time-consuming, and very expensive, although the staff in the small office of the large oncology practice where I get my chemotherapy are quite nice and very knowledgeable, and although I've met some very nice people who for the most part I would never interact with in my normal life (there is a real camaraderie among cancer patients, and much mutual support), I still don't find the experience very interesting or engaging. As a matter of fact, it's astonishingly dull. I bring books to read, but it's hard to concentrate, and I often find myself falling asleep, which has the advantage of making the time go by more quickly, and of off-setting the insomnia some of my medications induce.

2

I've written of HIV as "my doom before me," a destiny laid out for me the day that I was born, perhaps even before, since the virus might not have existed in 1963. Though I've not written much poetry about it, there is something both poetic and reproachful to poetry in HIV's literalization, its materialization, of the sex/death nexus so common as a poetic trope. It certainly has always made sense to me that pleasure could lead to death.

When I was diagnosed with HIV in 1994, it served more to confirm the sense I'd had since my Bronx ghetto childhood that I was destined to be destroyed by the world, a sense that my late mother, a very lonely woman terrified of losing me to the very things she aspired to for me, encouraged with her constant assurances that no one would ever love me but her. So it didn't really change my sense of self, and hasn't really been a major element in my poetry, though I'm sure that, like the death of my mother, about which I've also rarely written directly, it is a ghost presence in many poems.

There are poets who write powerfully about the experience of living with HIV and AIDS, and about its social and symbolic significance. In their very different ways, D. A. Powell, a gay man almost exactly my age, in his trilogy *Tea* (1998) ("dead boys make the sweetest lovers"), *Lunch* (2000), and *Cocktails* (2005), and the late Tory Dent, a heterosexual woman, in *What Silence Equals* (1993), *HIV Mon Amour* (1999), and *Black Milk* (2005) ("For seventeen years, I've said 'I won't live another year'") have done so. In the early days of the epidemic, the late Tim Dlugos addressed the topic in such poems as "G-9," about his experience in the AIDS ward of Roosevelt Hospital (for some reason this poem is not included in his posthumous selected poems volume, *Powerless*), and the late Paul Monette wrote his impassioned *Love Alone: Eighteen Elegies for Rog* (1988). Among writers who don't themselves live with HIV but who have written extensively about it, one can number Rafael Campo, the late Thom Gunn, especially *The Man with Night Sweats* (1993), Rachel Hadas, Eileen Myles, and Richard Tayson, and Aaron Shurin in the lyrical prose (including prose poems) of *Unbound: A Book of AIDS* (1997).

In part HIV hasn't been a major presence in my poetry because it hasn't been a major part of my life. I've had many medical crises since my HIV diagnosis, but most have not been related to my HIV status—my recurrent kidney problems, including painful kidney stones, are a major exception, since most seem to have been caused by various HIV medications I have taken over the years. I've been lucky in that I've had medical coverage and access to medications for this whole time, and my medications, whatever problems they've caused, have not had debilitating side effects, and have induced my HIV to behave itself like a good guest in my body—"I'm sitting here not bothering anybody. Don't mind me." That's the sort of relationship I want to have with HIV, if I must have one (and apparently I must). I hope that it will continue. I've often thought that if HIV were my only problem, even my only medical problem, I would be pretty damned well off.

3

My colon cancer, with which I was diagnosed and for which I had major surgery in November, and for which, because it has spread to my liver, I am now undergoing chemotherapy, has played a much larger role in my life. Besides the excruciating pain it caused me intermittently (pain that in retrospect I was lucky to experience, as colorectal cancer often presents no symptoms until it's too late to treat), I have had one major and one minor surgery because of it, with more surgery to come. In the first surgery, I was gutted like a fish to remove the golf-ball-sized tumor, the associated lymph nodes, and a portion of my colon (I believe that it's called a hemiectomy). In the second, I had a subcutaneous mediport installed for the efficient infusion of my chemotherapy medications.

I have recently completed my fifth round of chemotherapy, which is a major and intrusive part of my life. Every two weeks or so I spend several hours three days in a row hooked up to IV drips of various medications, spend two days carrying around an infusion of yet another medication attached to me by a thin transparent tube (during those days I can neither shower nor exercise), and then go in the following day for a shot to boost my immune system, which is already compromised by HIV, and which chemotherapy runs down even more.

All this is wearying and wearing, but not, for me, a source of poetic inspiration, though it may someday make good memoir material. In the meantime, I soldier on with the fatigue, the nausea, the diarrhea, the insomnia, and the inability to drink or touch anything cold, dreaming of the day when the tumors on my liver have shrunk sufficiently enough to be surgically removed, and I will be able to say goodbye, at least contingently, to the IV drips and infusion pumps, and will be able to drink anything I want at any temperature at any time. That will be a glorious day, a poem in itself.

By the time I was diagnosed with colon cancer, the sense of my own physical fragility and vulnerability had been pretty much pounded into me by my HIV diagnosis, my bout with Bell's palsy (especially frightening since there are no treatments if the facial paralysis doesn't end on its own accord), my subsequent hospitalization for a shingles infection in my inner ear which left me with only half the hearing in my right ear (the condition was so unusual that my doctor brought a gaggle of medical students to my room), my bouts with kidney disease and recurrent kidney stones (mostly caused by various HIV medications), the hearing distortion in my left ear which no manner of tests has been able to diagnose, let alone treat, an episode of secondary polycythemia, a condition in which one produces too many red blood cells which also earned me a hospital stay, since my blood was turning to jello and I was in imminent danger of a stroke, and my osteoporosis, because of which I've suffered several painful bone fractures. This is not to mention more mundane matters like my low testosterone and my high blood pressure (the latter has come down since I've started exercising and losing weight).

Cancer came as a highly unpleasant surprise, though it did explain the excruciating pain I suffered even after my lithotripsy to break up my most recent set of kidney stones. I have no risk factors, and I am more than five years shy of the age at which they recommend screening for colorectal cancer. But psychologically it just confirmed my sense of my body as frail and vulnerable at best, or set on betraying me yet again at worst. I've never really identified with my body, have always seen it as distinct and separate from, even in opposition to, my "self." It has felt more like a burden than anything else. Perhaps all these illnesses are my body's revenge, its way of reminding me that I am it and it is mine, it is me. What, after all, would I be without a body, however frail and ailing?

Who Can I Be Now?

In the interstices of being horribly sick (this was another chemotherapy week, with the usual panoply of crushing exhaustion, constant diarrhea, intermittent attacks of abdominal pain, continual nausea, and serial vomiting), I have been thinking about Lin Dinh's fascinating recent post "Our Bodies, Our Selves" (on the Poetry Foundation's "Harriet Blog," April 7, 2008), which begins by juxtaposing my recent litany of my various physical ailments with Kenneth Goldsmith's claims that an undefined "we" no longer have coherent selves, that "we're infinitely adaptable and changeable minute-to-minute." Lin Dinh's response to Goldsmith begins with these words: "Could someone with even a single serious illness believe that he can be 'everyone and no one at all'? That's he's 'infinitely adaptable and changeable minute-to-minute'? I don't think so. Hell, even a simple headache brings me back to my senses, reminds me of the limitations of my body and mind." I think that everyone is at least a somewhat different person in different situations, but I don't believe that people are wholly malleable. Nor do I think that anything is infinite, not even the universe: the most decentered self still has boundaries. But I can see the truth in both viewpoints.

We are all grounded in our bodies, in our immediate material existence. Some believe that such physical circumstance can be transcended, but it can't simply be escaped or ignored. At the

---

Editor's Note: Shepherd completed "Who Can I Be Now?" on April 13, 2008. The following day, he suffered a perforation in his small intestine, undoubtedly related in some way to his cancer or his cancer treatment, an incident which nearly killed him then. His recovery from that mid-April incident is discussed in the following two essays.

same time, we are as humans, as sentient beings, by definition not wholly confined by and determined by our immediate physical existence.

Some years ago I was walking down the street in Chicago with an HIV-positive friend while we discussed what HIV meant to us and to our lives. My friend insisted that HIV was who we were; I had to disagree. I am not HIV, and HIV is not me. In fact, I thought that we were two very bad examples of that viewpoint. My friend was and is a very talented painter; I was and am a poet. And in neither case did our work simply (or even complexly) revolve around our HIV status. That circumstance entered into our work, but didn't define it. My friend then suggested that it was only because we had access to HIV medications that kept the virus and its effects in check that we could see ourselves as separate from and in some ways independent of HIV, that otherwise, if we were dealing with its physical effects on a daily basis, it would be the meaning of our lives. Again, I had to disagree. Many quadriplegics, whose lives are about as circumscribed by their physical limitations as I at least can imagine, still nonetheless manage to lead lives that are not simply about being quadriplegics, whose meaning isn't that they are disabled. When I lived in Ithaca, New York, I had a friend from Norway who was confined to a wheelchair, having broken his back when he fell out of a tree. He was a musician and a music scholar, and his disability did not hamper him in his pursuit of his passions. He had even rigged up his car so that he could drive it with his hands alone.

I often think of the English painter and writer Denton Welch, who suffered a fractured spine from being hit by a car at the age of twenty and spent the rest of his short life in a wheelchair, dying in 1948 at the age of thirty-three. Despite his injuries, he went on to become a successful writer—the novel *In Youth Is Pleasure* is probably his best-known work—and the main influence on William S. Burroughs's work: Burroughs dedicated his novel *The Place of Dead Roads* to Welch (or rather, to the memory of Welch). I've no doubt that Welch's writing and painting made a great difference to his sense of self, especially at a time when to be handicapped as he became was more painful physically and socially than it is now.

The physical ailments I list in "Illness and Poetry" from which

Lin Dinh quotes have often been onerous (they are at the moment, while I am in the midst of chemotherapy side effects). But it is exactly the fact that I have other identities besides "a person with HIV" or "a person with cancer" that enables me to make it through my physical trials and travails. I am a writer, in more than one genre (poetry, creative nonfiction, literary criticism and theory). I am partner, lover, and friend to my darling Robert, who has transformed my life. I am someone who gets great joy from listening to a good performance of the love duet from *Tristan und Isolde,* as well as from hearing Kate Bush sing "This Woman's Work" or coming across a good Britney Spears remix. I am, when not suffering from nausea, a chef and a gourmand. And there are many other identities, more and less central to my self-definition, that I could list. It is by being all of these things at once that I am able to cope with having cancer, with having HIV, and with my many other medical conditions. If I were just my illnesses and their effects, I wouldn't be able to bear them for even a day.

If I may borrow one of Lin Dinh's identities for a moment, "I'm not here to express me, me alone[,] but as many selves as possible, including you if I'm lucky. . . . We don't have much of a choice but to entertain and bore each other with our bodies, our selves."

Long Hard Road Out of Hell

The short version: I was in the hospital for over a month, and almost died during the first week. According to my infectious disease doctor, by the odds, I should be dead.

The long version: Around April 14 I suffered a perforation of my small intestine which filled my abdominal cavity with unfriendly bacteria and led to a bad case of peritonitis, an inflammation of the intestinal tract. No one knows why or even exactly when the perforation occurred, so no one knows whether it might happen again, let alone how to keep it from recurring. The bacteria spread to my circulatory system, and I developed a nearly fatal case of septicemia, blood poisoning. I had three surgeries to clean out my abdomen over the course of ten days, including a resectioning that removed part of my small intestine (in addition to the portion of my colon that was removed in November along with my tumor) because it was irreparably infected. I was so swollen and distended that I couldn't be fully closed up after the first two procedures, because the internal pressure would have been too great. Before the first operation, my blood pressure collapsed (to something like 40 over 20), I had a heart attack, and my kidneys briefly stopped functioning; immediately after the second procedure, as I was coming out of anesthesia, I had a seizure. For quite a while I was on a ventilator, because I couldn't breathe on my own. The surgeon also discovered a bone fragment in my liver, probably the cause of some of my pain in that region.

I was unconscious or semi-conscious at most for all of this, so

Editor's Note: Shepherd wrote "Long Hard Road Out of Hell" and the following essay, "¿Tiene Dolor?," in late May 2008, just a few days after coming home from being in the hospital for five weeks.

I have no memory of these events. I only know they happened because Robert (and my doctors) told me about them. Indeed, Robert knows more about what happened to me than I do, since he was there, while I wasn't, at least not in any meaningful sense. I remember waking up at one point while Robert, who came to see me every day for as long as they would let him stay, was with me in the Intensive Care Unit, and asking how long I'd been there. "Two weeks," he replied.

That I could have died and not even known I was dying, not known that anything was happening at all, is terrifying to me, even more than the (quite terrifying in itself) knowledge that I almost died itself. There's an element of adding primal insult to injury in the thought that my own death wouldn't even be part of my experience, as if it weren't mine at all.

For me, writing all this down has the dual and perhaps contradictory effect of simultaneously bringing these events closer and keeping them at a distance; it serves both to internalize and to externalize what happened to me. Writing something down, achieving the mental distance to give it shape and form, is a way to gain control over experience, rather than be overwhelmed by it. But I didn't experience these things at the time; my knowledge of them is all after the fact. So writing this is also a way of making these experiences mine, of internalizing these events so that they become part of my experience. It makes them simultaneously more real (more mine) and less real (less crushing).

I've written before that I don't find being ill interesting, and illness is in general not interesting. But some of the mind's ways of coping with the body's utter helplessness are. I was very heavily sedated for the first two weeks or so of my hospital stay, largely for my own protection—so that I wouldn't, for example, try to rip the breathing tube out of my throat. (My wrists were in restraints for the same reason.) One strong effect of the sedation was to produce very vivid and often frightening hallucinations. At first, the hallucinations were distinct from reality, and I was often aware that I was in an hallucination. One involved playing a game based on the Disney animated series *Kim Possible,* about a high school cheerleader who also saves the world on a regular basis. I was on a high-speed train whose tracks were the ceiling tracks to which the hospital curtains were attached. If I could finish the game successfully, I would be able to escape the hallucination and get back to reality. But of course I couldn't, so I was trapped. I had another hallucination that I was in the car with Robert (I could sense his presence but I couldn't see or hear him—I spent a lot of time in my hallucinations looking for him, knowing that he was somewhere just out of reach), going from restaurant to restaurant all over town to compare their food, except that the windows were completely opaque and the car never moved. I was just stuck there, knowing that there was a world outside the car, but unable to reach it, though I could place orders for food I'd never get to eat or even see.

As I became more conscious, the hallucinations began to merge with the reality of my immersion in the Intensive Care Unit. This was a bad thing, as the lines between hallucination and reality became more and more blurred, and I could never figure out whether something was real or a delusion. I became convinced that, as in some horror movie in which an autopsy is performed on a man who is paralyzed but still alive, the hospital and its staff were trying to kill me. Robert tells me that they would ask if I wanted any pain medicine (I was in constant agony) and I would shake my head in terror, fearing what they might inject me with. He'd then ask me and I'd nod yes. That they gave me the shots despite my refusals further convinced me of their evil intentions. When the nurse took out the breathing tube on which I'd been dependent, I accused her of trying to kill me. When she denied trying to suffocate me, I cried out (with a strength that apparently surprised everyone) "You lie!" When Robert pointed out fifteen minutes or so later that I was still alive, I considered the situation, and then replied, "Sometimes it takes a while to die."

For much of this time I couldn't even talk, because of the breathing tube down my throat (at times I was partially paralyzed, doubtless by all the sedation). Even when the breathing tube was taken out, I could only manage a few whispered, labored words before being overwhelmed by exhaustion. I got a clipboard and some paper from the nurses and would try to write messages like "Don't kill me" and "I can speak," but they just came out as scrawls and scribbles, because my limbs were so weak and atrophied.

As the days went by and I became more lucid, I would test my delusions to see whether I had gotten back to reality. I became more fully aware of Robert during his visits, which was a great relief—as I wrote above, I spent a lot of my time while unconscious searching for him. (Robert tells me that even when I was unconscious I would occasionally wake for a few seconds, and if he was there I would touch and even grab him, to make sure that he was real. Sometimes I almost choked him.) I remember one day in particular during which I felt a great sense of relief—"Okay, this is actually real"—until something happened (I can't remember what) and I realized, "Oh no, I'm still in a delusion." When the random patterns on the acoustic ceiling tiles stopped looking as if someone had covered the tiles with every possible word or phrase (in several languages) that began with the letter "I" (including every pop song title imaginable), then I knew I had finally returned to reality, though prior to that day there were several times when I wanted to point out to Robert how clever whoever had created that ceiling palimpsest was. That, though, only takes me to about three weeks into my hospital stay, the rest of which was taken up with recovery and rehabilitation. And though I am finally at home, the road to wellness is long and winding. I have a large open wound along the entire length of my abdomen (it makes my colon surgery scar look like a little scratch), covered by a substantial dressing that must be changed by a registered nurse three times a week (a delicate and uncomfortable procedure). The wound is drained by a vacuum pump that is my newest and most indispensible fashion accessory; this must be detached and reattached each time the dressing is changed, and must provide an airtight seal. (The wound is apparently healing well—the nurses who've changed the dressing keep saying how "nice" it is.) And given the extent and intensity of my infections, I will be receiving daily intravenous antibiotic infusions into the foreseeable future—as of now, the medication has no stop date. Thanks to home health care, these are things that can be tended to in my own home. Thanks to a modicum of health insurance coverage, these are essentials to which I can actually (though just barely) afford access.

There is always the pain: dull, sharp, throbbing, stabbing, gradually building or suddenly overwhelming, ranging from the persistently uncomfortable to the excruciating. One day a physical therapist asked me, "Do you have pain?" I had to explain that the question isn't whether I have pain, but how much pain, what kind of pain, and where. Even with the various painkillers I've been on continuously since my admission to the hospital, painkillers I'm now in the process of trying to wean myself from, since they're addictive and also cause constipation of epic proportions, I've yet to have a day free of pain. It's only recently that I've had any extended respites from pain. But though the pain subsides, it never entirely goes away. There is also the exhaustion brought on by the simplest household tasks, like walking from one room to another, due to the atrophying of my limbs after a month of lying in a very uncomfortable hospital bed. I spent a substantial amount of my time and energy in the hospital learning how to sit up again, how to stand again, how to walk again, regained skills which I now practice many times a day just going from one room to another in my house.

I don't know how to end this piece, especially given that the story hasn't ended—I don't know how things will turn out, though I'm told that I'm healing well. Perhaps that optimistic note is the best place to stop.

¿Tiene Dolor?

Pain is my constant companion. This has largely been the case for over a year, with all my emergency room visits, operations, and hospital stays. But since my abdominal perforation and the month-long hospitalization and three surgeries it entailed, pain has never left me. Pain that would have seemed unbearable two years ago now often seems merely a baseline level—unpleasant, uncomfortable, but not requiring any extraordinary measures. Only what my oncologist calls "breakthrough pain" is worth special notice.

Each time I've had some episode of overwhelming pain for hours and hours at a time, I've writhed around thinking or crying out, "I can't stand it, I can't take it anymore." And each time I've discovered that I can indeed bear it, that I can take it. This isn't a discovery I would have liked to make. All my illnesses, along with the various other crises in my life, have made me realize that I'm a much stronger person than I thought I was, physically and psychically. But I would have been happy never to have known how strong I could be, never to have been put to that test, even though it's a test I've passed over and over. One gets no prizes for passing it, though I suppose that having survived this most recent incident when many people wouldn't have is a reward in itself.

Every room in the hospital had a little chart pinned to the wall with which one could measure one's pain in a range from one (no pain) to ten (excruciating pain), accompanied by a series of round faces that went from a rather overly-perky smiley-face to what was supposed to be a picture of great, if cartoonish, suffering. "Are You in Pain?" the poster asked. Or as I always read it, "Are You into Pain?" In Spanish, it would ask, "¿Tiene dolor?" Have you sorrow, have you grief? Why yes, I always thought, I do.

The nurses and other medical personnel would periodically ask what my pain level was, using the numbers on the chart. I tended to exaggerate, naming a slightly higher number than I felt, knowing that if I described my pain in the terms of someone who had become as acclimated to it as I had, they would dismiss it, not take it seriously. I tend to be fairly stoic about physical discomfort, and what would seem excruciating for most people is rarely so for me, not now anyway. Nonetheless, my felt pain level would rarely be lower than halfway through the chart—if it got down to four, that was a very good day indeed.

Concomitant with my ability to bear a great deal of pain is a persistent resistance to pain relievers, with which I've been afflicted since I was a child. When I would go to the dentist for the very extensive work I had back then, I had to be so pumped full of novocaine that I'd be numb for the whole day and sometimes into the next. (I began getting symptoms of Bell's palsy facial paralysis in 1996 on a day when I'd been to the dentist, and at first I thought that the limpness on one side of my face was a lingering effect of the novocaine, until I realized that I couldn't blink either.) Pills in particular do very little for me. Under its various names, Vicodin, Lortab, etc., is about as effective as sucking on a Ricola lozenge, except that it doesn't taste very good. And so on up the line, Percocet, Demerol (more effective than most), etc. Even Dilaudid pills, which are supposed to be very potent, do very little to alleviate my pain.

I don't drink, I don't smoke, and I don't take drugs, nor have I ever, but during my recent lengthy hospital sojourn I began to understand something of what an IV drug addict must feel when he or she shoots up and the drug hits her or his system. While oral Dilaudid is almost ineffective for me, intravenous Dilaudid relieves my pain quite quickly, though the effect is rather short-lived. I well remember many occasions lying in my bed in great pain waiting for the nurse to bring my pain medicine (everything in hospitals happens in slow motion, except when they decide that they're going to take you down for a CT scan *now*), sometimes twitching and crying out.

If the nurse gives a Dilaudid shot too quickly, pushing it in all at once, it causes dizziness and nausea, but if she gives it slowly and properly diluted with saline solution, after a moment it produces a wave of calm and well-being that washes away the pain as it flows over one's body. The feeling is fairly fleeting, but it's a wonderful release after one has been crushed in pain's grip. I imagine it's the closest thing I'll ever know to that "rush" or "high" that IV drug addicts experience, and it makes me understand a little why they are so desperate for it. That "Aah" of release and relief is my only fond memory of being in the hospital.

So no, I do not have pain. But pain has me, and will not let me go.

Heaven Is a Place Where Nothing Ever Happens

On Tim Dlugos's "Turandot"

I am in the hospital for the fourth time in the past five months, this time for excruciating abdominal pain that turned out to be due to a bowel obstruction which has still not cleared up. I have had a tube down my throat and have been unable to eat for over a week. I spend most of my days trying to sleep through the pain and nausea.

In the course of the various tests to try to determine the cause of the obstruction, my surgeon found several large masses on my liver which, after a blood test and a liver biopsy, have turned out to be a fast-growing resurgence of my colon cancer. Thus I am in the hospital cancer ward for the foreseeable future, starting chemotherapy again (it had been on hold during my assorted medical crises of the past few months), before I have had time to fully recover from my recent illnesses and surgeries.

Doug Powell recently wrote on the Poetry Foundation's "Harriet Blog" about the late gay Tim Dlugos, which reminded me of one of my favorite of Dlugos's poems. It's one of the last poems Dlugos wrote before he died of AIDS in 1990, and my recent brush with death has made it particularly resonant for me.

Editor's Note: Shepherd wrote "Heaven Is a Place Where Nothing Ever Happens" from his hospital bed in late August 2008, about two weeks before his death from the aggressive cancer that had returned sometime between late July and mid-August.

When I try to imagine
what heaven will be like,
I think of Puccini's Pekinese
court, ruled by a big Joan Sutherland
type wearing an enormous headdress,
where riddling has metastasized
from a show of wit into a burning
passion, consuming all the time
that passes in the progress
toward an end that never comes,
and everyone, not only the sympathetic
slightly ridiculous Ping, Pang and Pong,
has long since been sated by the marvels
of the capital, and just wants to go home.

In keeping with the this-worldliness of Dlugos's sensibility, its insistence on the preciousness of the things of this world, "Turandot" is an ironic meditation on ideas of the afterlife, imagining heaven as the rather warped imperial Chinese court of Puccini's opera, in which the titular virgin princess (recorded by, among other sopranos, Joan Sutherland) subjects each of her suitors to a set of three riddles, and executes all those who cannot answer correctly, which turns out to be all of them. (Really, the riddles aren't that hard. But perhaps all these princes are too addled by love to keep their heads.) As the comic courtiers Ping, Pang, and Pong complain in the opera, life has been reduced to three bangs on a gong, three riddles, and one head chopped off. This is how Dlugos pictures heaven, as a place where nothing happens, over and over again forever.

Whereas the opera ends with Turandot's heart finally being melted by Prince Calaf, who answers the three riddles and whose true name, she realizes, is love, in the poem's heaven there is no end to the riddling, to the pomp and ceremony and ritual. There's a clear allusion to and an implied critique of the ceremonials of organized religion, specifically the elaborate rituals of the Catholic Church in which Dlugos was raised, and of the religious emphasis on the life to come as opposed to the earthly life which is the only life we know we have. At the end of this rather brief poem, everyone, having had more than their fill of the wonders of Peking, simply wants to go home. But of course there is no home to which one can return after death, no going back to earthly life. Thus the poem also implies a critique of the Christian notion of the resurrection of the body, and of all the ideologies that convince us to value an imagined or potential afterlife over the actual life we are living. So "Turandot" is a veiled *carpe diem* as well (Calaf tears off Turandot's veil to melt her heart with his kiss), which warns us to seize the day and live in the now. As the opera tells us, there are three riddles, but only one death—and only one life.

What's in a Name?

Steven Burt's January 2008 post, "All-Name Team," on the Poetry Foundation's "Harriet Blog," and the posts I did in February here on "Reginald Shepherd's Blog" on gay poetry post–identity politics, have had me musing about identity, social and personal, and about the role names play in producing identity. I've been thinking about names, what they are and what they do. As Burt points out, poetry is a kind of naming, and naming is in turn a kind of poetry. In poems, names are like magic talismans that contain and convey the essence of the thing named. So when two things are given the same name, then they are or become the same. And when the name changes, then the thing named changes.

The thought of changing names and things, in turn, has me thinking of my own name (everything makes me think of me), the changes it has undergone over the course of my life, and a couple of people with whom I share that name, whom I'm quite sure are not the same, as me or as each other. But when I look myself up, there they are. And when I look up the wrong spelling of my name, some other version of me, there I am anyway, as if I were two people who've led the same life, or at least who've published the same things in the same places. As Burt points out, "Titles, names, labels ask questions, and raise possibilities." So who are the possible me's my name makes possible?

Editor's Note: Shepherd wrote "What's in a Name?" in early August 2008, in between hospital stays. In mid-August, a couple weeks after writing the essay, a couple weeks before his death, and back in the hospital again, he was baptized Reginald Alexander Shepherd.

1

I was born Reginald Berry on the morning of April 10, 1963. Berry was my unmarried mother's last name; like the protagonist of Diana Ross and the Supremes' "Love Child," I started my life in an old, cold, rundown tenement slum, burdened by the stigma of illegitimacy, which for me was the same as poverty. The birth certificate I am always losing documenting the birth of "Reginald Shepherd" was issued in 1968, after my mother had sued my deadbeat Barbadian father to prove that he was indeed my father. What we got out of that I never understood, since he almost never paid the meager thirty-five dollars a week in child support as ordered by the court.

I sometimes wonder if who I am changed when I ceased to be Reginald Berry (I was five) and became Reginald Shepherd: indeed, when I ceased ever to have been Reginald Berry. Reginald Berry was erased, as if he had never been, and his place was taken by Reginald Shepherd, as if I had always been him and he had always been me, except that Reginald Shepherd came into existence at the age of five, having completely bypassed birth and infancy, not to mention the terrible twos and threes.

I was enmeshed in the social services network at a very early age (as everyone in her family always said, my mother knew how to work the system), and to this day I am in the Social Security Administration records as Reginald Berry Shepherd, a name I have never legally had or even gone by, a name that has never been mine. They remember all the pasts, and conflate them into one.

Would my life have been different if I had remained Reginald Berry, if Reginald Berry had not been erased as if he had never existed? At the least, people would have much less occasion to misspell my name, and who knows what effect that confidence that I would be correctly spelled could have had on my self-esteem?

My mother (who went from being Blanche Berry to being Blanche Graham—my stepfather's name—without ever having been Blanche Shepherd) always told me that my name meant "Great King" in Celtic. According to the Online Etymology Dictionary (whose only authority is that of its author, Douglas

Harper), my name derives from Old High German and means "ruling with power." According to Dictionary.com Unabridged (which bases its claim to authority on the *Random House Unabridged Dictionary*), it derives from an Old English word meaning "counsel and rule." I believe that it's related to the name of the Celtic goddess Rigantona, whose name means "Great Queen." Someone in college told me that my name was the ablative form of the Latin *rex*, "king," meaning something like "of or from the." Perhaps I was the king's favorite shepherd or, in my previous life, his favorite fruit. My younger half sister is named Regina (my mother had a plan); her name unambiguously means "Queen." I confess to being a bit jealous of her name's indisputable authority.

But despite the grandeurs of my first name, I have felt a little deprived that I don't have a middle name. My mother had one, later my abusive Jamaican stepfather had one, and still later my younger half-sister had one. I settled on "Alexander" as an appropriate middle name: Alexander the Great was a famous king and conqueror, and the initials "RAS" spelled out the Amharic word for "prince." (The late Emperor Haile Selassie I of Ethiopia was known as Ras Tafari Makonnen, "Prince Tafari Makonnen," before his ascension to the throne. Hence the group name Rastafarian, though this quasi-religion has never had any connection with Ethiopia.) But I never had my name legally changed, and as I got older I lost interest in the matter.

2

The name Reginald has very different connotations for white people and for black people. For white people, the name sounds very English, and my Anglo accent, though one that I can't hear, often makes them inquire as to whether I am English, or perhaps West Indian. I just reply that I got my accent from my Barbadian father (whom I met once) and my Jamaican stepfather (who abused my mother and me). But almost the only people in America nowadays with the name Reginald are black. It's become an almost quintessentially black name, like Antoine (often spelled Antwan, or Antuan) or Leroy/Leroi ("the king").

Mine is one of a set of categories of black names. There are the names that white Americans don't use anymore, like Cedric or Tyrone, names that have been handed over to black people (though in the hospital I did have a white physical therapist named Tyrus—but then, the South has always been a bit backward). There are also names like Reginald, Maurice, or Roderick (this last one is on the edge) which have become predominantly black names but aren't yet perceived so by white people. There are the made-up names, like Materia, Tawanna (a cousin of mine—she was meant to be named after the Mexican border city), or Chicalaundra (pronounced "Shalandra"). There are the Frenchified names, like LaQuan or LeVante or LeBron or LaToya (also LeToya), or the (male) driver of the Greyhound bus I used to take to work when I lived in Chicago, LaHarry. I remember joking once with a black friend that you can make any name black just by adding "La" or "Le" to it; then I realized it was true. ("De" will also work, as in DeWayne, DeMarcus or, my favorite, Da'Sean, pronounced "DAY-Shawn"—the apostrophe makes all the difference.) Then there are the faux-African names, like Kechia/Keshia/Keisha, Kena (another cousin of mine), Kima, and Kwame (this last a genuine West African name appropriated by black Americans). There is an overlap between Frenchified black names and faux-African names, as in Lakeisha or Deshondra, and between the made-up names and the faux-African names, like Tawanna or Kima or Ebony/Eboni. There are also the Arab names, like Jamal and Malik, Omar and Raheem/Raheim. I've always found black Americans' tendency to give their children Muslim names odd, since Muslim Arabs were major slave traders for over a thousand years. A category which seems to have dwindled are names taken from words of rank and position, so that a white person calling a black person by (usually) his first name would still have to show respect, even if the act was meant disrespectfully. The singer Prince a/k/a "Symbol Thing" (born Prince Rogers Nelson) and poet Major Jackson would be examples. Mine is also an example of such a name, since, as I wrote earlier, my mother always told me that it meant "Great King."

When I was a kid, and up until my mid-twenties, I went by "Reggie." The only other two Reggies I knew of in my childhood were the baseball player Reggie Jackson and the Archie comic books laughingstock rich bad boy Reggie Mantle. He once went into an office and, unsatisfied by the secretary's refusal to be impressed by him, announced, "Someday my name will be a household word," to which her response was, "Like dirt?"

A few months before my twenty-fifth birthday, I decided that I was too old to be called "Reggie." That was a child's name, and it was time for me to put aside childish things. Since then I have gone by my full name, though people still insist on calling me "Reggie" and "Reg." But even when I went by Reggie, already a shortened version of my name, many people insisted on calling me "Reg." Besides the obvious fact that it wasn't my name (if I wanted to be called Reg, I would introduce myself that way), as my oldest friend Merav's mother put it, "Reg" has the air of a hale fellow well met, a football player perhaps, and that's never been me or anyone I wanted to be. I've never understood why people would need to nick a nickname, anyway. Some people still call me Reg, and I always correct them, except for my editor at the University of Pittsburgh Press, Ed Ochester. He has loyally published me for many years, so if he wanted to call me "Joe," that would be all right with me.

3

Because I am not devoid of pride, and because I always want to know whether I'm being talked about and what people are saying if I am, I periodically look myself up online or, as they say, "google" myself. (Perhaps "Google" should be capitalized, since it is a trademark.) The only other Reginald Shepherd who comes up is an aged and very Caucasian Canadian painter, a self-described "poetic realist" who seems well-known in his native Newfoundland and in neighboring Nova Scotia, but nowhere else as far as I can tell, even in Canada. I think of myself as a kind of poetic realist as well, in life and in my poetry, so perhaps our kinship is more than name deep.

Years ago, when I lived in Chicago, another, decidedly less savory Reginald Shepherd popped up when I searched myself. An apparent career criminal (all that came up were his various arrests), he was something of an evil doppelganger. I was once almost denied an apartment because of my arrest for "criminal shoplifting" (I always wondered what legal shoplifting was) in 1991, two years before I moved to Chicago. And once I received a letter from a social service agency informing me that some woman I'd never met had named me as the father of her child. I had to call and explain that the last time I had been in the vicinity of a woman's vagina was the morning I was born. One of the other Reginald Shepherd's old addresses, in an area of Chicago I would never have ventured into, even appeared on my credit report, an error (among several others) it took several calls and letters to rectify. My criminal double has either settled down into legal respectability or died (either is equally likely), as he hasn't shown up in my web searches for several years. I would like to think that he has seen the error of his ways and become a law-abiding citizen, but I have no great desire to inquire further.

The most common misspelling of my name is the transformation of my last name to Shepard, which people sometimes insist upon doing even when they're publishing or paying me, no matter how many times I sign and print the correct spelling of my name. It doesn't seem to matter that my last name is a word, as in "German" or "the Good," though I did once see a sign pleading for the return of a lost "German shepard" dog, which may be a testament to people's general inability to spell. Oddly enough, people almost never misspell my first name, perhaps because it's relatively uncommon and so they don't assume that they know how to spell it better than I do, thus leaving only the correct spelling.

Given how frequently my surname is misspelled, I will sometimes do an Internet search for "Reginald Shepard." Besides finding various references to my misspelled self, which I try to correct when I can, I also come upon references to a death row inmate in Florida by that name. I don't know what his crime was, but I imagine that it was probably murder. I find it a little disturbing to once again have a criminal doppelganger living (though who knows for how long) in the same state. At least there are two crucial letters separating my name from his, his fate from mine. But still . . .

UNDER DISCUSSION
Annie Finch and Marilyn Hacker, General Editors
Donald Hall, Founding Editor

Volumes in the Under Discussion series collect reviews and essays about individual poets. The series is concerned with contemporary American and English poets about whom the consensus has not yet been formed and the final vote has not been taken. Titles in the series include:

On Frank Bidart: Fastening the Voice to the Page
edited by Liam Rector and Tree Swenson
On Louise Glück: Change What You See
edited by Joanne Feit Diehl
On James Tate
edited by Brian Henry
Robert Hayden
edited by Laurence Goldstein and Robert Chrisman
Charles Simic
edited by Bruce Weigl
On Gwendolyn Brooks
edited by Stephen Caldwell Wright
On William Stafford
edited by Tom Andrews
Denise Levertov
edited with an introduction by Albert Gelpi
The Poetry of W. D. Snodgrass
edited by Stephen Haven
On the Poetry of Philip Levine
edited by Christopher Buckley
James Wright
edited by Peter Stitt and Frank Graziano
Anne Sexton
edited by Steven E. Colburn
On the Poetry of Galway Kinnell
edited by Howard Nelson
Robert Creeley's Life and Work
edited by John Wilson
On the Poetry of Allen Ginsberg
edited by Lewis Hyde
Reading Adrienne Rich
edited by Jane Roberta Cooper
Elizabeth Bishop and Her Art
edited by Lloyd Schwartz and Sybil P. Estess